Good Job!

A Young Person's Guide to Finding, Landing, and Loving a Job

For Robert,
You've been part of the team at Y.E.S. which made this book possible. I hope it can help a young person you might know. Thanks for all your support for Y.E.S. Keep up the good work! Best wishes.
Nancy

Nancy Schaefer

Stoddart

Published in 2000 by Stoddart Publishing Co. Limited
34 Lesmill Road, Toronto, Canada M3B 2T6
180 Varick Street, 9th Floor, New York, NY 10014

Distributed in Canada by General Distribution Services Ltd.
325 Humber College Blvd., Toronto, Canada M9W 7C3
Tel. (416) 213-1919   Fax (416) 213-1917
Email cservice@genpub.com

For information about U.S. publication and distribution of Stoddart Books, contact 180 Varick Street, 9th Floor, New York, NY 10014

04 03 02 01 00 1 2 3 4 5

Canadian Cataloguing in Publication Data

Schaefer, Nancy
Good job!: a young person's guide to finding, landing, and loving a job

ISBN 0-7737-6109-8
1. Job hunting. 2. Youth — Employment. I. Title.
HF5382.7.S323 2000 650.14'0835 C00-930029-5

Cartoon Illustrations: Greg McEvoy
Cover Design: Bill Douglas @ The Bang
Text design and typesetting: Kinetics Design & Illustration

The Canada Council for the Arts since 1957 | Le Conseil des Arts du Canada depuis 1957

We acknowledge for their financial support of our publishing program the Canada Council, the Ontario Arts Council, and the Government of Canada through the Book Publishing Industry Development Program (BPIDP).

Printed and bound in Canada

For all the young people
who are looking for jobs, and
the people in employment agencies
who help them

Contents

Preface

How is this book different?

If you are young and looking for work then this is an essential book for you. While people of all ages find job searching a challenge, the difficulties facing you as a young person in Canada looking for work are unique. Now, finally, here is your own book.

Good Job! was written with lots of participation from young job searchers just like you. And like you, they wanted a book that is useful and relevant to the difficulties young job searchers face. So this book speaks in plain language, gives straightforward advice, and has all the basic information you will need to find a job.

Many youth looking for a job have thoughts like:

No one will hire me.
What's wrong with me?
There are no jobs that I want to do.
Finding a job is too difficult and I don't know how.

Lots of people have these doubts, and if you share their feelings, know that you're not alone. Follow the steps in the pages ahead. They provide the answers you'll need to get a job. No matter how desperate your situation may seem now, it will get better. You will get a job.

Yes, feeling alone in your job search is common. But this book will also show why you don't have to do it alone. It helps you seek out the support of your friends, family, or guidance counsellors, and how to find an organization in your community that offers free job-search advice and training. There is even a short chapter on how to find these community-based agencies near to where you live. Employment centres can save you a lot of time, give you someone to talk to, and take away the feeling that you are alone.

Why do I feel like this anyway?

Finding work isn't easy, especially if you don't have much work experience or a college or university education. Parents and society can put pressure on you because you're not working, making you feel like you're "goofing off," or that you're a "slacker." You know it's not true. The problem is they just don't understand how hard it can be when you're first starting out in the world of work.

I wrote this book to encourage you to believe in yourself. You will get a job. Most of us want the same things: to be happy, to make some money, to feel fulfilled. Don't let pressures get you down. Finding a job is hard, but it's not impossible.

Look on the bright side . . .

Being young and looking for work has its advantages. Remind yourself that you have lots to offer an employer. Think positive thoughts, like:

I'm young and full of energy.
I'm creative and have fresh ideas.
I can learn new things.
I'm flexible because I have fewer responsibilities.
I feel like I can do just about anything.

There is a job for you and this book will help you get it.

Good luck!

Acknowledgements

I mentioned in the preface that this book was written with the help of young people, most of whom are job seekers who understand what you're going through. I want to thank all the members of the many youth focus groups who gave their opinions and advice freely and generously.

Special thanks go to the youth members of the Book Advisory Team, Christine Lambert, Laura Shilliday, and Duc Phan. They have worked hard to ensure that the language, content, and style of the book are youth focused, understandable, and accessible. Their participation in the book's development was critical.

Most of the information in this book was provided by the staff at Youth Employment Service (Y.E.S.) in Toronto. I want to thank each of them for their input and their ongoing belief in the value of every young person who makes their way to our organization. We understand that regardless of the state of Canada's economy — boom, recession, or somewhere in between — young people need help to find a job.

Y.E.S., with the generous assistance of Human Resources Development Canada, the Ontario Ministry of Training, Colleges and Universities, the City of Toronto, The Rotary Club of Toronto, and many other individuals, foundations, and corporations, has helped over 33,000 youth to find work since 1968.

I want to thank my colleague, Jonathan Bennett, who provided the inspiration for this book. His belief in the importance of this project has never wavered and he has given me the constant editorial support necessary to make this book a reality.

Thanks also go to my two teenage daughters, Victoria and Amanda, for giving me the opportunity to appreciate youth culture and to understand the highs and lows of teenage years.

My appreciation goes to Marnie Kramarich, senior editor at Stoddart Publishing, for having the vision to publish this book; Sheri Hebdon, who helped co-ordinate many aspects of the project at Y.E.S.; the Y.E.S. board members for their support — in particular, Geoff Dean and Chris Snyder; and the Raptors Foundation, The K.M. Hunter Charitable Foundation, and The McLean Foundation, who all believed in the book and provided assistance.

Finally, I would like to thank The Atkinson Charitable Foundation. The Foundation gave generous support and their executive director, Charles Pascal, gave me interesting and innovative ideas.

I owe a great deal of gratitude to the many people who have made this book possible.

Nancy Schaefer

1

Starting Out

"Hey! I need a job."

Each year, in every province, many thousands of young Canadians come to the very same conclusion: "Hey! I need a job."

If you're one of them, then you're probably feeling all sorts of things right now. Along with realizing that you have to — or want to — look for a job come many different emotions, like the excitement of new experiences and the thrill that you'll be earning your own money. But for some people who have not had much work experience, the idea of job searching can also be a little scary.

If you're feeling scared, or frustrated, or you don't know where to start — or if you're worried that no employer would hire someone like you — then you've come to the right place. Deciding that it's time to get a job means you want to take action. So let's get at it.

Will having a job mean I'm different now?

There's no doubt about it: working will affect your life in many new ways. Working is not like school. At work, people expect different things from you; you'll also discover different rewards, feel different pressures, and experience different successes and achievements.

What can a job do for me?

Having a job, whether it's a part-time job during the school year, a summer job, or a full-time job after you're done with school, is a great way to gain the respect, freedom, and independence you deserve.

Having a job will give you money to buy the things you need and want. It will help you pay for your life. You will be able to help others around you, like your parents, girlfriend or boyfriend, siblings, or roommates, because you'll be taking better care of your own needs.

Here's what some young Canadians have said about their first year at work:

> *"I like it. I work in a restaurant three nights a week. It's hard sometimes, long hours. But the tips are pretty good. I'm saving for a car."*
>
> — Brendan, age 18, Fredericton, NB

> *"I worked in a store last summer. My uncle got me the job. I have to make money for university."*
>
> — Eva, age 16, Montreal, QC

> *"I'm working as a labourer. I work for one guy who owns a small landscape company. It's just me and him. In the summer we do*

yard work. Winter we plough snow and do other odd jobs. We get along pretty good. When I dropped out of school, he just hired me. He took a chance on me."

— Joe, age 17, Hamilton, ON

"I help out my mom and dad on the farm. I've always done it. But now that I'm older it's changed things a little. I have to do it, not just when I feel like it."

— Jenny, age 15, North Battleford, SK

"My older brother started a business designing web pages and I help him. He works full-time and I work part-time, full-time in the summer. It's been going for almost a year now. I like working from home but he pays me only when he can — it's hard starting your own business at the beginning. But I'm just doing it for the experience because I want to be a computer programmer."

— Sanjay, age 16, Richmond, BC

So as you can see, there are many, many different types of jobs. Some young people work part-time during the school year, others work only in the summers, while some have finished with school and are working full-time.

What jobs can I do?

The secret is to discover what you are already good at, what you already enjoy doing, and start looking there.

Warning: As someone just starting out in the workforce, you'll find that it's hard to get that "dream job." Sure, we all know that lucky someone who seems to have the best job going, but job searching is all about planning and being realistic.

Yes, it's a better idea to take a job that you want rather than just any job. But it's not always that easy. For some, the money — getting a paycheque — is the most important thing, and the sooner it arrives, the better. If that's you, then take the first job you can; but remember, your future is open and you don't have to accept "just any job" for long. For now, work and earn that money you need. But keep looking. Your dream job *will* come one day, and the most important step to getting it is to start somewhere. That's where you are right now.

Your first few jobs will give you important experience to move toward your dream job or help you build a fulfilling career. Even if you don't know yet what the dream job is, every job requires experience. Now is the best time to begin to build it. So let's get started.

It's important to know your skills and interests. Even if you've never had a job before, you still have many interests and skills that employers will look for.

A quick three-step guide to focus your job search
Ask yourself:

1. **What kinds of jobs do I find interesting?**
2. **Why do these jobs interest me?**
3. **What am I already good at?**

Here are some other questions to help you decide what kinds of jobs you might like to do:

Do I like working with people?
Do I like working with my hands?
Do I like working with computers and technology?
Do I like working in a team?

Do I prefer working on my own?
Do I like working during the days or at night?
Do I mind working on the weekends?
Do I like working outside?
Do I like talking to people on the phone?
Do I like convincing people and selling ideas?
Do I like to read a lot?

What kinds of jobs do other youth get?

Here is a list of typical jobs for young people in Canada. Of course, the jobs vary from province to province and from season to season, but this is a good starting point:

- Retail jobs in shops, mall stores, department stores, grocery stores, movie cinemas, superstores, gas stations, video stores.
- Service jobs, such as waiter/waitress, table busser, cook, host/hostess, bell hop, front desk attendant, server, cashier, kitchen support worker.
- General labouring jobs, which might involve painting, window cleaning, cutting lawns, snow removal, leaf removal, house cleaning, landscaping, labour at building sites, warehouses, and factories.
- All kinds of short-term jobs found through temp agencies.
- Summer jobs, such as lifeguard, parks and rec. worker, landscaper, camp counsellor, tree planter, tour guide, house painter, amusement park worker, child care worker.

- Office jobs, such as filing clerk, telemarketer, web designer, secretary, receptionist, data entry clerk, administrative assistant, word processor.
- Government jobs. Many government departments hire young people for both summer and permanent work. Check out the government web sites, or ask a guidance counsellor or employment counsellor.

TEMP AGENCIES are companies that find short-term work assignments for skilled workers by matching them with employers who need help for just a few days or weeks. If you are interested in joining a temp agency, look in the Yellow Pages under "employment."

Deciding on what kind of job you would like to do can be tough, but the choice is yours to make. Take control of your job search. It's not just a matter of filling out applications and waiting by the phone for employers to call you back. You can take steps to make sure you get those calls!

When you narrow down what kind of job you would like, it's time to do a little research. Ask around, check out the Internet, and find out more about the areas you are interested in. How do other people get jobs in those fields? It's up to you to discover the many ways to get what you want.

RESEARCHING a job means to gather information about a position. This includes finding out about duties, responsibilities, pay, location, and hours of work.

Why do young people get jobs?

Young people get different types of jobs for different reasons. Here are some:

- to make money
- to get experience
- to get respect
- to save for a car
- for something to do
- to have freedom
- to be independent
- to save for school
- because friends have jobs
- to pay rent and bills
- to save for a trip
- to learn about a potential career

I don't have any idea what kind of job I want!

Don't worry if you can't decide on the kind of job you want to look for. It happens to everyone. In fact, most people question the kind of job they want many, many times in their life.

Because working is still pretty new to you, and you haven't experienced work life for long, it's hard to decide what you might like to do. If this is you, then here are some options:

- Get some job advice from an employment agency. (Check out chapter 10 of this book for help in finding a centre near you.)
- Do a general job search and see what you can find. Who knows, once you get started, something you see advertised might appeal to you.
- If you have a few different possibilities but can't narrow it down, ask someone you know if you can spend some time "job shadowing" them. Job shadowing means you spend an hour or two with someone on the job to see first-hand what is involved in that position. Perhaps a friend is doing a job that you might like. Ask them to ask their boss if you can hang out for a while and help so you can see if the job appeals to you.

What is a part-time job?

Some students who live at home with their family get part-time jobs during the school year to gain work experience. Other students are saving for things they want, like a car, or a holiday, or money to go to college or university. Still other youth in school work just to earn some spending money. Many students take jobs for a combination of all these reasons. Working part-time after school or on the weekends just makes good sense.

What is a summer job?

Almost all students fill their summer holidays with work of some variety, even if it's volunteer work. Having a summer job is a great chance to gain experience in the workforce, make new friends outside school, and, in most cases, earn money. Some students focus on getting jobs that will help them learn about careers they might like to pursue later on, while others are simply interested in making as much money as they can while school's out.

What is a full-time job?

Whether it's before or after graduation, at some point everyone finishes with school. The next step is either to get more education or to get a full-time job. If you feel like school is not where you want to be at the moment, then full-time jobs are necessary because they give you the money to support yourself, pay rent, buy food and CDs, and even to save a little. When you're not in school, working full-time makes you feel good. It gives you a steady income, lets you plan ahead, and gives you the power to take control of your life. It's hard to get by if you're not in school and don't have a full-time job. Some people even get more than one part-time job to give them full-time hours.

A full-time job can give you the opportunity to plan and save. It's a great way to get what you want.

What is a volunteer position?

A volunteer job is an unpaid position. It gives you on-the-job experience that will help you get a paying job later. It can also help someone in need, or benefit animals or the environment. Volunteering is very important because it shows that you care about your local community, and it gives you skills and experience. If you are not going to get paid work right now, or if you feel you have some extra time, then the best thing you can do is to volunteer. It makes you and those around you feel good, and employers love to see it on a résumé.

What if I'd rather work than be in school?

Everyone tells you to stay in school, right? But are they really right? Is it right for *you*?

If you've dropped out of school, you'll know this is true: getting a full-time job without a high school diploma is not easy. It's not impossible — people do it every day — but don't be fooled, it is hard.

It's hard because so many people in Canada have a high school diploma and that makes the competition for jobs very tough for those without one. It's even a minimum requirement for many entry-level jobs.

ENTRY-LEVEL JOBS are positions that require the least amount of previous work experience or education.

Also, the kinds of jobs you can get with a high school diploma are often much higher paying and are probably better jobs than those you can get without one. It's just a fact of life.

Whether it's right or wrong, many employers believe that staying in school shows that you can finish something, that you can complete something you started.

So if you can, stay in school. But if you can't, plan ahead. Talk to your parents, or older brothers or sisters, or a guidance counsellor about your future after school. Ask them to help you think about what you want to do after high school is over for you. Start thinking about it now. You can't even begin to imagine all the many different courses offered at community colleges. Look at some material in the guidance office. Surf the web and look up colleges in your area. Find out what it takes to get there. Yes, getting an education is expensive, but it'll pay off in the end. Dream a little . . . it'll come true if you want it badly enough.

If you can't stay in school, if you simply must have a job and money to support yourself now, then don't despair. Read this book and collect your thoughts. There is a job out there for you and it will help you get the things you need like money for rent and food and clothes. Start looking for a job today. Once you know how and where to look, you won't believe how many employers need someone like you.

The good news is that there are many youth employment centres right across Canada that will help you find a full-time job. (Check out chapter 10 of this book for help in finding a centre near you.) They have people there who are experts in helping young Canadians like you find full-time work . . .

- even if you didn't finish up to grade 12
- even if you're not sure where you want to work
- even if you're supporting a child
- even if you don't have a résumé

- even if you've never really had a job before
- even if you've left home
- even if you're new to Canada
- even if you have a criminal record.

The staff at youth employment centres will help you take many of the steps outlined in this book, so give the centre nearest you a call. Searching for a job can be hard if you're new at it. You don't have to do it alone.

2

Preparing for a Job Search

"Where do I start?"

There are a few basic things you'll need to have ready before you can begin to look for a job. Take the time to get them in place before you start and avoid hassles later on.

Checklist — The Basics:

- **a Social Insurance Number (SIN)**
- **a phone number with an answering machine**
- **references**
- **time set aside for job searching**
- **a positive attitude**
- **a nice set of clothes for interviews**
- **access to help for your job search, if needed**

Do I need a Social Insurance Number, or SIN?

Everyone should have a Social Insurance Number (it's called a SIN for short). It's a form of identification necessary for getting a job. A SIN is a nine-digit number, given to you on a plastic card. When the Government of Canada gives you your number, it allows you to work because you'll need to give it to your employer when you get hired. The SIN is used for your taxes, employment insurance, and pensions. You might also need it for other things like applying to get into college, university, or other types of further education.

How do I get a SIN?

There are several ways you can get an application form for a SIN. The best is to go to your local Human Resources Centre of Canada (HRCC) office and pick up an application. You can find the one nearest to you by looking up "Social Insurance Numbers" in the Government of Canada section of your local phone book. It's the "blue pages" section. Also, you can call and ask to have an application form mailed to you, or you can download it from the web site of Human Resources Development Canada (HRDC), which is the ministry that oversees all the HRCC offices in Canada. You could also ask a friend who already works where they got their application form.

After you've filled in the form, follow the instructions carefully. You will see that when you return to the office to hand in the form, you will need to bring documentation proving your identity and status in Canada. It is also possible to mail in your application and supporting documents. There is no fee to apply for an initial SIN number.

For more information call your local HRCC office or visit HRDC online at the following web site: www.hrdc-drhc.gc.ca

Remember, a SIN is a private number. You are not legally required to give it to an employer until you are hired.

What if I never get my telephone messages around here?

A reliable telephone number, with an answering machine hooked up to it, is extremely important while you are job searching. It is important for an employer to be able to reach you at any time and leave a message if you are not home. Make sure the "greeting" you have on the machine is basic and professional. While you're job searching it's best to avoid humorous messages.

If you share the telephone with other people, tell them you are job searching. Make sure they know how important it is that you get your messages promptly. They will need to take down all the details: the caller's full name, the time they called, any message they left for you, and a number where you can call them back.

If you do not have a telephone number, there are many youth employment services that can set you up with a voice-mail number while you are job searching. (Check out chapter 10 for help in finding a centre near you.) Also, you could ask a friend to let you use their number while you are looking for a job.

What are references?

A reference is someone who agrees to speak to a potential employer about you and your abilities in a positive way.

What is a reference letter?

A reference letter is a professional letter written by a previous employer, teacher, coach, or someone else who can honestly speak about your skills and abilities. Most employers will want to speak directly to your reference; however, some might also accept a reference letter.

★ **TIP Always make photocopies of a reference letter to give to employers. At an interview, have the original with you in case the employer asks to see it, but let them keep only a photocopy.**

It's always a good idea to ask your supervisor for a reference letter when you leave a job or volunteer position. This is especially true if you know it will be difficult for an employer to contact your reference in the future.

Who should I choose to be my references?

The best reference is your last employer. They know better than anyone how you performed on the job. This is why, where possible, it is important to leave a job on good terms and ask for a reference letter.

How can I get references if I'm looking for my first job?

Most employers who are hiring for entry-level positions understand that young people don't have much or any work experience and therefore won't have previous employers as references. If this is your first job search, a reference can also be a teacher, a coach, clergy, or someone you volunteered for. The important thing is to ask someone who knows you and thinks highly of you.

Who cannot be one of my references?

A reference cannot be someone who is related to you. This includes your parents, uncles, aunts, cousins, siblings, step-parents, and grandparents. Girlfriends or boyfriends are also not appropriate references. Even using a friend is not recommended. An employer will only be impressed by positive comments about you if they come from someone who does not feel obliged. Whatever you do, never use someone who shares your address and phone number.

When you give your references to an employer, you have to say what your relationship is to that person, and when that relationship occurred. Don't lie.

If you can't use a previous employer, or you don't have one, it's best to pick someone older than you, and someone who has supervised you in some way, like a teacher, youth worker, or coach.

What will a reference need to say about me?

A reference will have to be able to tell an employer that you are (for example) . . .

- a good person
- a hard worker
- reliable
- honest
- punctual
- trustworthy
- a fast learner.

A reference is not a character witness. They have to be able to give concrete examples of your skills and abilities. Choose someone who has supervised you in some way. It's best if they have known you for a number of years.

Is it a big deal to ask someone to be a reference?

Yes, and you will find people will want to be honest. So choose someone you like and who likes you. Most importantly, ask their permission. Here's how you might want to approach a potential reference:

- "Hi, Ms. ___________, it's ___________ ___________. I'm about to start looking for a job as a _____________. I was wondering if you would mind being a reference for me?"

Tell your references you will call them and let them know when you have an interview. Keep them informed of your job search.

TIP Not only is it polite to warn a reference when they can expect a call — it's to your advantage. A reference who knows about the specific job you're applying for is more prepared and is more likely to answer an employer's questions with examples that are well thought out.

When do I have to give my references?

Some employers insist on references being listed right when you first apply on an application form, while others won't ask for them until an interview. Not all employers check references, but most do. That's why it's best to be prepared with your references before you start your job search.

How long will my job search take?

It's difficult to say because everybody is different: a few days, a week, perhaps months. It will take time, but if you stick with it and follow the advice in this book it will shorten the time it takes. You'll get that job.

It's a good idea to keep a list of all the places you contact in your job search. Keep track of the names of the companies and the people you talk to when you visit or call, because employers may keep your résumé "on file." This means that if you don't get the job this time, they will keep you in mind for a future position. It's not uncommon to receive a call from an employer weeks, even months, after you dropped off your résumé. So keep note of the places where you've applied. If a potential employer calls you back, you'll want to remember where they are located and who you talked to there.

What if I'm too busy right now to look for a job?

It takes a lot of time to get a job. As you'll often hear people say, "it's a full-time job getting a job." Make sure you have the time. Sure, sometimes we get lucky and find success on the first day. But, sadly, this is not usually the case. Putting in an hour or two a week won't be enough.

Also, when you start getting interviews, it takes time to get to where the interview is held, and time to get home. Make sure you leave yourself enough time on the days you have interviews. You don't want to be rushed or show up late.

Most importantly, make sure you are ready to start, and that you have time to work. Having a job is an important commitment. When you are scheduled to work, you have to be there. You can't just miss a day for no good reason. Make sure that if you accept a job, working will not get in the way of any other important commitments you may have, like school. You can't be in two places at once.

★ **TIP** **Job searching needs a positive attitude. You will get a job. You must stay at it and try your best. It will happen. Look around you at all the people who go to work every day. At one time, they were in the same position as you are. They made it, and you will too. If you can prepare for some rejection, it'll be easier to continue on until you hear those words: "I'd like to offer you the job." If you think you are good enough for the job, an employer will, too.**

How much will my job search cost me?

Job searching costs some money. Although there are employment centres you can go to for free help and services, such as free Internet access, free faxing, and free newspapers, job searching can still cost money. If you take the bus, it costs money to get to an interview. To buy a nice set of clothes for interviews will also cost money. If you are having financial difficulties with your job search, be sure to contact the nearest youth employment service provider near you. They can often arrange for free transportation to interviews and provide you with access to clothes for interviews.

What if I don't have an address or phone number right now?

If you are living temporarily away from home, on the street, or in a shelter, you still have options. There are many free services that can help you search for a job. They can often help you get connected to housing services and social assistance in your community, and get you a free phone number and voice mailbox to use while you are looking for work. There are always options; in most cases, all you need to do is ask. Read chapter 10 of this book for help in finding an employment service near you. There are experts ready to help you find a job if you can't manage it on your own. Everyone knows that finding a job is hard when you're young. The important thing is to ask for help.

What if I really need money today?

Job searching takes time. It's a simple fact that for most young people, job searching means facing some rejection. That's why it's important to keep at it and to not give up. It's common for youth looking for first jobs to only get one interview for every twenty résumés they submit. And that's just getting an interview. Actually getting a job may take several interviews. This might seem discouraging, but look at it another way — getting good at interviews takes practice and now your skills have improved.

If you need a full-time job today because you are desperate for money to pay rent or buy food, call a nearby employment centre today. They can get you connected to government programs that will help you if you're in urgent need.

★ **TIPS**

- Get started as early as you can. Take the first step as soon as possible.
- Have a positive attitude. You will get that job.
- Following the advice in this book will help you get a job sooner.
- Rejection does not mean you won't get a job, or that you are not a capable person. Rejection happens to everyone, and it's a normal part of job searching.
- Have a reliable phone line with an answering machine, and remind your friends or family to take detailed messages while you are job searching.

3

The Application Form

"Don't I just have to fill it out and give it to them?"

Think of the application form as the first step to getting an interview. Take it home and fill it in carefully. Then, return the application, paper-clipped together with your résumé and cover letter, to the employer. Including a résumé and cover letter (see chapters 4 and 5) is an extra step but it may put you ahead of the other applicants. It shows your interest in the position is serious.

What is an application form?

An application form is a sheet, often double-sided, that is used by employers to check out potential candidates for a job. Application forms are tools to help employers obtain some basic information from you and ask you some simple questions about yourself, your employment history, education level, and other qualifications.

Will every job that I want to apply for have an application form?

No, but many entry-level, part-time, and summer positions do and so it is important to know how to fill them in correctly.

Employers that typically use application forms include summer camps, government, retail stores, restaurants and fast food outlets, warehouses, factories, temp agencies, pools, amusement parks, video stores, cinemas, and telemarketing companies.

The good news is that application forms are easy to obtain, and they treat each potential candidate equally.

How do I get an application form?

Most places that use application forms require you to apply in person. Stores, restaurants, and government offices will all have application forms available for you to pick up. It's a good idea to call the employer before you go in and ask if they have application forms to fill in.

What should I say when I get there? What if I'm too embarrassed?

It sometimes feels difficult to just go up to someone who is working and ask for an application form. But lots of people do it every day. Once you've asked for one application form, you'll see it's no big deal and it just takes a second.

Who should I speak to?

Most employees can give you an application form but the best plan is to ask to speak to the manager. So keep in mind that even when you're just picking up the form there is a good chance that you will meet the person who does the hiring. Dress nicely, smile, and be sure to introduce yourself to whoever gives you the form. You want to make a strong first impression. If they remember you, it might be what gets you an interview later.

★ **TIP Find out the name of the hiring manager. Write it down and get the correct spelling. You're going to need it when you're writing your cover letter. If you forget to ask while you're picking up the application form, call them back later to find out. You might say something like:**

"Hi. My name is _________ _________ and I picked up an application form earlier today. I'm just about to do a cover letter and I wonder if you could tell me the name of the hiring manager?"

TIP Collect the application form from the employer and take it home. Don't fill it in nearby and drop it off twenty minutes later. Filling in an application form takes time to do well and it must be done neatly. Also, that way you will be able to customize your résumé and cover letter for each different application you make. Standard résumés and cover letters are impersonal and are not as successful as those that have been written specifically for each application.

What will I need to know when I'm filling one out?

Correct contact information

This means your name, address, and phone number (which is connected to an answering machine or voice mailbox).

Other information
Application forms frequently ask you to name the schools you've attended and describe any previous positions you've held. Be sure to include volunteer positions. *Warning:* You will need to know when you started and finished working your previous jobs.
Hours of availability
Try to be as available as you possibly can.
Names and phone numbers of references
Although it is not recommended to give out names of references on your résumé or cover letter, application forms sometimes ask for them. If this is the case you can write "available on request" in that space and, if you get an interview, bring along a sheet listing your references, or copies of your reference letters if you have any. If you choose to include them on the application form, remember to ask permission from your references first. Tell them that you are job searching and filling out applications and that they may receive a call.

But doesn't my résumé say all this again?

Yes, there will be some overlap between your résumé and the application form, but you must go to the extra trouble. Filling in an application form does not replace the need for a résumé or cover letter. You should still hand in all three. They are all equally important and doing this will really increase your chances of getting an interview.

LOOK AT IT FROM THE EMPLOYER'S POINT OF VIEW

If an employer at a store in a mall receives fifty-four application forms, one of the ways he or she will separate them into "yes" and "no" piles is by looking at how completely, neatly, and accurately the applications are filled in. An employer definitely wants an employee who can follow the simple instructions on the form and looks organized.

Ten Steps to Completing a Successful Application Form

1. Be prepared and look professional.

When you go out to pick up application forms, look your best. Bring along a notebook or pad of paper, plus a pen. You should keep track of every employer you visit and every employee you talk with. It'll help you remember if you don't hear back for a few weeks.

2. Smile and be polite.

When you go into the place where you want to apply, ask if you can speak to a manager. Be very polite and speak clearly. If the manager doesn't want to be disturbed, then just direct your questions to the person you are already speaking with.

3. Ask for two application forms.

Again, be very polite and ask if you can have two application forms. You can say something like: "I'm interested in applying for a job here. Is there an application form?" If there is an application, then say: "I'd like two copies if possible please." If you can't get two, then photocopy the form before you begin to fill it out. That way you'll have one to practise on first.

4. Get as much information as possible.

Finding out more about the workplace will help you decide if this is the right job for you. If the person you're talking to seems friendly and isn't too busy, ask them about the position. You could ask if they know when they will be scheduling interviews, or how many hours they expect people to work. If they are busy, it is best to keep it short. Just make sure to get the name of the manager in charge of hiring.

5. Take the application home and fill it out.

Do a thorough, very neat job. Make sure to get help from a friend or parent when filling out parts that you aren't sure about.

6. Attach a résumé and cover letter (see chapters 4 and 5 for more help).

Even if the employer doesn't ask for a résumé and cover letter, do them anyway. It will make you look more organized. Try to include in your cover letter any information you collected when you picked up the application.

7. Return the application directly to the person doing the hiring.

Before you return your application, call first. If you weren't able to find out the person's name when you picked up your application, this is also a good time to find it out. Handing your application directly to the person doing the hiring will improve your chances of being chosen for an interview.

8. Remember the name of the person who took your application.

If the person in charge of hiring is not available, don't worry. Write down the name of the person who takes your application. Call back later or the next day to speak to the person doing the hiring and say, "I brought in my application yesterday and gave it to ____________ ____________ . I just wanted to make sure you received it."

9. Don't try too hard, or annoy the manager.

If you're calling just to see whether or not they got your résumé, try not to ask for any other information. Hopefully you already know when they're doing the hiring. If not, that should be the only other thing you ask at this point. Don't ask for details about the job. You don't want to bother them and hurt your chances.

10. Call back to check on your application a few days before they said they'd be interviewing.

It's okay to call the person you know is in charge of hiring just to say, "I just wanted to check on my application." It will be clear that you are interested and that you're organized enough to have kept track. This will give a great impression at the critical time when they are deciding who to interview.

Warning: If you are told "Don't call us, we'll call you if you are chosen for an interview," or something similar, don't call. Always follow the employer's instructions.

What questions should I ask when I'm handing in the application form?

Here are some good things to ask and say when you're handing in your application. When you first drop it off, you might say:

- "Hi. I'm __________ __________. I'm dropping off my application for the __________ position that is available. Can I please speak to the person doing the hiring?"

If you manage to get introduced to the person doing the hiring, try asking some questions:

- "Can you tell me a little bit more about the position?"
- "Do you have any idea of when you will be scheduling interviews?"

If you have an opportunity, tell them you are interested in the position:

- "As you'll be able to see from my application, I'm really interested in the position. This looks like a great place to work."

Always remember to dress nicely, smile, shake the manager's hand firmly, and confidently thank them:

- "I appreciate your taking a few moments to speak with me. I hope to hear from you soon."

What if they ask a question that I think is private or personal?

In Canada, there are laws that govern the relationship between you and your employer, and they take effect and begin to protect you even before you are hired, when you are applying for jobs. Although the laws differ from province to province, you always are guaranteed certain rights.

If you think an employer has asked you an unfair question on an application, call or visit the web site of your province's ministry of labour and find out. You can find the phone number in the "blue pages" of your phone book or by doing a search on the Internet. Know your rights.

Some applications just ask weird questions. If you come across a question that you think is irrelevant or strange, all you can do is try your best to answer it.

DO'S AND DON'TS OF APPLICATION FORMS

✓

- *Do take the form home and fill it in neatly, in blue or black pen, with no spelling errors.*
- *Do have someone you trust look it over for you.*
- *Do attach a cover letter and résumé.*
- *Do try to speak to the person doing the hiring whenever you can.*
- *Do dress well when you are handing in your application form.*
- *Do keep track of the places where you've applied.*

✗

- *Don't ever lie on an application form.*
- *Don't leave any parts blank, or questions unanswered.*
- *Don't write, "See attached on résumé." Always fill it out in full.*

I need more help with my application form . . .

If you need more help with your application form, your nearest youth employment centre can help you. Check out chapter 10 of this book for help in finding a centre near you. Also, remember that you can ask a friend, parent, or teacher to give you a hand. It's always a good idea to ask for some help when filling out application forms.

4

Résumés

"Do I really need one?"

Yes. Résumés are an important part of any job search because most employers insist on them as part of the application process. Whether you are looking for a part-time, summer, or full-time job, a well-written résumé will help you achieve success. Some young people worry that writing a résumé will be hard because they lack experience. That's understandable, but everyone needs a résumé, and they're not hard to write once you know how. Tell yourself that you can do it and that there is a job out there for you. Once you've written one résumé, it gets much easier.

What is a résumé?

A résumé is a short summary of who you are, what you have done, and what you can do. This includes your skills, abilities, work history, volunteer experience, education level, interests, and strengths. A résumé also states your full name, address, phone number, and, if you happen to have them, your fax number and e-mail address.

The good news is that your résumé should not be longer than one or two pages. If you have never had a job, or your work experience is limited, then one page is all that you need.

How should I start writing my résumé?

A great way to start thinking about the kind of job you might like to apply for is to simply start doing your résumé. Sitting down and writing your résumé will help you see exactly what it is you have to offer. Take a look at some sample résumés on pages 43–46 to get an idea of what a finished one looks like.

Now, start by making a list of all the different experiences you have had in school, after school, during the summers, and on weekends. Include all previous jobs, sports, volunteering, hobbies, clubs, and anything else you can think of. Next, make a second list of the skills and attributes that your experiences show. For example, you may be hard working, a team player, dedicated, a strong communicator, able to do many tasks at once, responsible. Once you've built a list, you're ready to begin!

I wrote a résumé last summer. Can I just use it again?

Because you change over time, so must your résumé. As you accomplish new things, your résumé should grow and change. Never just send off an old résumé. Always add in the new skills and experiences you've gained since the last time you wrote it. You will change your résumé over the course of your lifetime many, many times. Start now. In fact, with each new job you apply for, you should take a good look at your résumé and customize it.

★ **TIP** **When updating your résumé, remember to customize your cover letter too.**

How do I make my résumé reflect what an employer is looking for?

Ask yourself the following questions:

Are the contents of my résumé in the best order?
Are the most applicable experiences and skills listed first?
Have I left out anything that would help me get the job?
This includes volunteer experience, hobbies, and interests.

What should my résumé look like?

There is no "right" way to set up a résumé. A résumé should reflect who you are and what you do. How it looks is totally up to you but it must always be clean and neatly organized and it must honestly reflect your experience and skills. Also keep in mind that employers expect to find certain things on your résumé, and they expect them to be presented within some basic guidelines. But you do have a choice.

There are three basic types of résumés to choose from. The first two types are very standard résumés, and the third is a newer type — a combination of the other two types — that many young people choose. Take some time to decide which one of the three will best highlight what you can offer an employer.

Chronological résumés

A chronological résumé is the traditional type of résumé that lists your experiences by date. It is divided into sections such as work experience, education, volunteer experience, achievements and awards, and hobbies and interests. Your work experience should be listed in order, with the most recent position appearing first.

If you are looking for your first job, or you have not had a lot of work experience, this is probably not the best type of résumé for you. This style of résumé suits older workers who have been in the workforce for some years. It gives a history of their work experience. It is especially good for showing strong commitment to a company or organization. This is the type of résumé you will likely want to work toward in a few years.

Functional résumés

Because functional résumés emphasize skills and downplay lack of experience, they are great for young people who are looking for their first job, or who have not had many jobs. This type of résumé focuses on skills gained in volunteer work, hobbies, and sporting or extra-curricular activities.

Combination résumés

If you've had some work experience, but not a lot, you might want to choose to do a combination résumé. This is an approach that combines the best from both types of résumé styles mentioned above.

There is no doubt about it — employers like to see work experience, so if you only have a little (one or two previous jobs) then the combination résumé might be for you. On it you can list, as in a chronological résumé, your previous work experience, but you can also, as in a functional résumé, show the skills that you gained in other activities. For many young job searchers with a little work experience, this option is the most successful.

What goes into a résumé?

Name and address

No matter which style you choose, at the top of your résumé you should place your full name, address, and phone number in bold and slightly larger type than you use for the rest of the résumé. If you have a fax number or e-mail address, you can list these as well.

★ **TIP** **Remember to have a working answering machine, with a short, polite message, hooked up to your phone line while you are job searching. Inform your family, or the people you live with, that you are job searching. Tell them it is important that you receive detailed messages. If you have an e-mail address and you decide to list it, make sure it is straightforward (like john_smith@internet.com or jsmith123@hotnet.ca — no slang or silly nicknames) and check it often. Listing your e-mail address is a good idea because it tells an employer that you are computer literate.**

Career or job objective statement

It is a good idea to include a statement of your career or job objective at the beginning of your résumé only if you are:

- applying for the same position at many different places. For example, if you want to work as a waiter or waitress and you are applying to many different restaurants, or you want to work as a salesperson at a store and are applying to many different stores

  or
- planning to drop off your résumé to many different places.

In these cases, having a clear, straightforward objective is helpful because it tells an employer, at a glance, what kind of job you are interested in. This is especially true if there is no application form to fill out, or you do not intend to do a cover letter. (See chapters 3 and 5 for information on application forms and cover letters.)

Most employers receive many résumés, which they put in a pile until it comes time to hire. That's when an objective statement helps an employer choose which candidates to interview.

Sample Objective Statements

- **To obtain a full-time summer position working in retail**
- **To obtain a part-time position working as a prep cook**
- **To obtain a full-time position working in customer service**

Remember, if you decide to change the kind of position you are applying for, you must change your objective statement. Don't make the mistake of faxing a résumé with the objective statement "To work as a waiter" to a company that is hiring a receptionist.

TIP Objective statements are not as effective as a cover letter that is written specifically for the job to which you are applying. Employers respond much better to the extra effort you demonstrate when you write a cover letter. Also, for tips on how best to approach employers, look at the chapter on application forms.

"Highlights of qualifications" or "summary of skills"

In a big pile of résumés, this section is a great way to quickly tell a busy employer about your strongest skills and qualifications. Your summary of skills should appear at the top of the page, just below your name and address, and it is usually written as a list.

Your experience

You're probably thinking, "It's hard to write a résumé when I don't have much work experience." That's true, but here's a way around it: consider a functional résumé. Check out the example on page 45. It is most important, as a new job searcher, to de-emphasize your lack of work experience and incomplete education and to emphasize the skills you've gained in other areas of your life at school, at home, or in your community. What you don't have

in work experience you do have in personal qualities, and this will convince an employer that you possess the qualities they are looking for, such as creativity, "being able to learn new things easily," and trustworthiness.

Work experience (no job too small)

If you've had a job or two, be sure to list them, even if they were only short-term. Even a part-time job for a few days or weeks is good work experience. You will need to show the name of the company, organization, or person you worked for; your position or title; the dates you worked; the company's location (city or town); and a description of the duties and skills you gained on the job. Check out the examples on pages 43–46.

★ **TIP If you worked for only a short time, simply list the month, or the season, that you worked.**

Volunteer experience

Volunteer experience is very important to anyone looking for a job, but it is especially important for you if you don't have a lot of work experience. It's never too late to start volunteering. A volunteer job gives an employer an indication of your interests and what you care about. Volunteer experience can be listed in a separate section or along with any work experience. Be sure to list the following:

- the name of the person, charity, or non-profit or community organization you volunteered for
- your position or title
- the dates you volunteered
- the general location
- a description of your duties
- a list of the skills you gained

Volunteering is excellent work experience to showcase on your résumé. It shows that you are someone who cares about your community and that you are willing to spend your own time to help others.

The skills that can be learned in volunteer jobs are also highly valued because they often require attractive qualities like . . .

- dedication
- caring
- understanding of other people's needs and wants
- an awareness of a larger community.

If you have never volunteered, you don't know what you're missing. Get involved with a cause or charity that is important to you. You'll feel good about yourself, help someone who is in need, and one day it might even help you get a job.

★ **TIP If you're listing volunteer experience in the same section as paid work experience, call the whole section "relevant work experience" so you are not misleading the employer.**

Education

It is important to list the schools you have attended and which grades you've completed or your expected year of graduation. If you have graduated, then be sure to list the diploma earned. It's a good idea to list specific courses that you enjoyed or did well in. It shows an employer your interests and strengths. If it's applicable to the position that you are applying for, be sure to list any relevant courses. For example, if you are looking for a job where you will be working with cash, and you have completed a math course, then be sure to list it.

Awards and achievements

If you have any awards or achievements, be sure to list them, even if they are not directly relevant to the position. They show an employer that you have been successful and recognized by others. Awards and achievements can be from many different areas of life and they show that you are well rounded. They could include any of the following:

- sports championships, team awards, other awards
- academic scholarships, awards, high grades, honour roll
- life-saving levels, CPR certification, swimming levels
- any licences that you may have obtained — driving, flying, boating
- any language that you speak fluently

Hobbies and interests

Almost everyone has hobbies or interests. They are a great way to show an employer that you are good at different things. Who knows, an employer may share your love of computers, or dance, or chess, or hockey. Hobbies and interests show you as someone who is outgoing, interested in learning, dedicated, and focused. Try not to repeat your awards and achievements in this section.

★ **TIP** Don't list any hobbies or interests that won't help you get a job. "I am an avid reader" or "I enjoy many sports" or "I love to cook" are good, but "I like to watch TV" or "I love shopping" or "I love to go clubbing" or "I like to hang with friends" should be avoided.

What style of résumé should I pick?

It's up to you, but here are some guidelines:

- Your résumé should be on either standard plain white, off-white, or very light grey 8 ½" x 11" paper.
- Always type your résumé. If you don't have a computer, ask a friend if you can use theirs or go to your local employment resource centre (for help in finding one, read chapter 10 of this book). NEVER write your résumé by hand.
- Use the same font style and size as your cover letter. Keep it simple.
- Single-space your résumé, keeping a double space between sections.
- Bold your name at the top, and repeat your name in the header of the second page, if you have a second page.
- Be sure to spellcheck your résumé, and have someone you trust read it over to make sure you don't have any spelling or grammatical errors.
- If you are applying to a specific industry, ask someone you know who already works in that industry to look over your résumé.

How should I send my résumé?

If you are responding to an advertisement that gives instructions on how the employer wishes to receive your application, then always follow the instructions. Respect an employer's wish for no phone calls if that is their request.

If they leave it up to you, or you are responding to a "help wanted" sign or a lead from a friend, or you are taking initiative and simply forwarding your résumé, then follow the basic guidelines on page 58, in the section on cover letters.

DO'S AND DON'TS OF RÉSUMÉ WRITING

✔

- ***Do list other languages you speak if you are going to be dealing with the public. Candidates with more than one language are an asset to companies and organizations because they can provide better customer service.***
- ***Do list all the computer programs you know.***
- ***Do have someone you trust proofread your résumé for spelling mistakes and grammar.***
- ***Do use professional wording; for example, "child care" sounds better than "baby-sitting."***
- ***Do send a clean, neat, and tidy résumé.***

✗

- ***Don't list your date of birth or your social insurance number or references.***
- ***Don't attach a photograph of yourself unless it is specifically required.***
- ***Don't print your résumé on coloured paper. Use only white, off-white, or light grey.***
- ***Don't send a résumé that has been photocopied so many times that it is blurry or crooked on the page. Print a fresh copy that has been updated with your latest skills and experience.***
- ***Don't ever lie, mislead, or inflate your actual skills and experience.***
- ***Don't overdo fonts, boldface, underlining, or italics.***
- ***Don't squish your résumé onto one page if you have enough to fill a second page. A second page is fine as long as you don't have too much white space left over at the bottom.***

Sample résumés

The pages that follow contain several sample résumés. Take a good look at each of them and then decide which is most like the one you want to create for yourself. Work with it and make yours great and truly your own.

- See pages 42 to 44 for examples of the most common style of résumé for young people — the *combination résumé.* The first sample résumé is a blank outline you can use as a guide.

- See page 45 for an example of a *functional résumé.* It is a good style to choose if you have very little or no work experience, as it de-emphasizes work experience and education.

- See page 46 for an example of a *chronological résumé.* This is the traditional style of résumé that is best used if you have completed your education and have a solid work history over a few years.

> Type your name in bold.

> Make sure you include your fax number and e-mail address if you have them.

YOUR NAME
Street Address
City/Town, Province, Postal Code
(xxx) 555-5555
Fax: (xxx) 555-5554 e-mail address if you have one

Highlights of Qualifications or Summary of Skills

- ______
- ______
- ______
- ______

> List achievements, accomplishments, and important skills that relate to the job you're applying for.

Skill Grouping 1

- ______
- ______
- ______

> Group your skills into categories and give them headings, such as "Clerical," "General Labour," or "Customer Service."

Skill Grouping 2

- ______
- ______
- ______

> List "one-liners" that describe how and when you used or gained each of these skills.

Skill Grouping 3

- ______
- ______
- ______

> List all your previous jobs, including volunteer positions, starting with your most recent position.

Work History

Years worked	Position	Company Name	City / Town
___ to ___	______	______	______

Education

Years attended	Grade/Diploma	Name of School	City / Town
___ to ___	______	______	______

References available upon request

> List your highest degree or diploma first.

WILLIAM JACKSON
41 West Street
Toronto, Ontario
M5A 6L3
(416) 555-9286

HIGHLIGHTS OF QUALIFICATIONS OR SUMMARY OF SKILLS

- Trustworthy, responsible, reliable
- Works well with others or independently
- Able to complete tasks within limited time
- Committed employee
- Experience handling cash and cheque transactions
- Able to use a variety of landscaping equipment responsibly and safely

RELEVANT SKILLS AND ABILITIES

GENERAL LABOUR

- Operated gas-powered lawn mower and trimmer
- Loaded and unloaded equipment from truck
- Worked over sixty hours a week and maintained productivity
- Hauled away trimmings and debris

CUSTOMER SERVICE

- Maintained good relationships with clients by always being friendly and polite
- Helped company grow by asking clients for referrals
- Collected payments and issued receipts
- Called clients to verify that rain dates were convenient

WORK HISTORY

1998 to 1999	Landscaper	Grasscutters	Toronto
1997 to 1998	Landscaper	J & T Landscaping	Toronto

EDUCATION

1999	Diploma	MacDonald Secondary School	Toronto

References available upon request

JOANNA STEPHENS
723 Ellis Avenue
Halifax, Nova Scotia
B3J 6K2
(902) 555-2961 jstephens@freemail.com

HIGHLIGHTS OF QUALIFICATIONS OR SUMMARY OF SKILLS

COMPUTER LITERATE

- Able to work with minimal supervision
- Able to work as part of a team
- Excellent communication skills
- Professional and courteous

OFFICE SKILLS

- Answered phones on multi-line system
- Transferred calls to extensions or voice mailboxes
- Operated fax machine, photocopier, credit card authorization system
- Fast and accurate typing abilities
- Able to use a computer for word processing and data entry
- Performed light bookkeeping duties

CUSTOMER SERVICE SKILLS

- Worked at front desk and greeted people coming in
- Used polite phone manner
- Dealt with client complaints or directed them to appropriate person
- Promoted upcoming sales and/or events

WORK HISTORY

1998-present	data entry/back-up receptionist	MDL Systems Inc.	Halifax
1997-1998	cashier	Angie's Fashions	Halifax

EDUCATION

1996-1998	William Lyon MacKenzie S.S.	Halifax

References available upon request

RICHARD JONES
Box 23
Outlook, Saskatchewan S0L 2K3
(306) 555-1913

SUMMARY OF SKILLS

- Can do many tasks at once
- Committed to seeing things through
- Hardworking and dedicated
- Easily adapts to different environments
- Learns new tasks quickly

SKILLS & EXPERIENCES

GENERAL LABOUR

- Lifted over 60 lbs for extended periods of time
- Operated various types of farm equipment
- Performed building maintenance tasks: roof repair, caulking, eavestrough cleaning
- Interior and exterior painting

SALES

- Managed table at local farmers' market
- Set wages according to current prices
- Bartered effectively to attain best prices for goods
- Performed quality control checks on food being sold
- Gave proper change during cash transactions

ANIMAL CARE

- Tended to over 150 animals within limited time span (before school)
- Assisted with birthing of new pigs and sheep
- Since 1995, member of Youth 4-H
- Ensured safety of animals by proper fencing and gating

EDUCATION

1998 to present Outlook High School Outlook, Saskatchewan (to graduate 2002)

References available upon request

JENNIFER ALDERMAN
63 Westchester Street
Winnipeg, Manitoba R5T 2K4
(204) 555-4726

HIGHLIGHTS OF QUALIFICATIONS:

- Hardworking, honest, and reliable
- Experience dealing with children
- Good problem-solving skills
- Can do many things at once
- Good with people

RELEVANT EXPERIENCE:

1997-present **Caregiver**
Falcon Family, Winnipeg, MB

- Care for two children under the age of 5 without supervision
- Prepare meals and snacks
- Plan activities for children
- Supervise when friends come over to play

1995-1997 **Mother's Helper**
Falcon Family, Winnipeg, MB

- Assisted with care of newborn baby — feeding, changing
- Played games with two-year-old while mother rested
- Made sure all toys were put away properly
- Taught two-year-old how to say the alphabet

EDUCATION:

1999-present **Lester B. Pearson Secondary School**
Winnipeg, MB

- Expected date of graduation: Spring 2004

References available upon request

LOOK AT IT FROM THE EMPLOYER'S POINT OF VIEW

You finished your résumé! Great. But make sure you don't stop there. A very important thing to know about making a résumé is that once you get a general version finished, you should be prepared to change your résumé slightly for each different job you apply to. This is also true for cover letters. Employers will respond more favourably and this will greatly increase your chances of getting an interview.

Where to get more résumé help

Résumés can be difficult to write when you're starting out. Almost everyone, at some time in their life, has had to write a résumé. Ask around. Try a teacher, guidance counsellor, family member, or youth worker. Also, keep in mind that there are professionals at youth employment centres who can help you write your résumé. Most services are completely free. Check out chapter 10 for help in finding a centre near you.

5

Cover Letters

"Do I always need a cover letter?"

Writing a cover letter might seem like extra work, but remember — you want that job. A cover letter is a chance to make a good first impression. It's the first small step to showing an employer that . . .

- you're the best person for the job
- you can do the job
- you want the job.

It will never, *ever hurt* you to write a cover letter. Employers will rarely say in an ad, or in person, "Be sure to write a cover letter." That's because it's expected of you. "Drop off your résumé" always

means that you should also attach a cover letter. A good cover letter will give you an edge over the other applicants.

Cover letters and résumés are different. They can tell the employer different things about you. Think of a cover letter as a very short advertisement or commercial for yourself. It does not just repeat what is on your résumé. A cover letter introduces you and your résumé, and it's an opportunity to state your strongest points and show an employer why you are the right person for the job.

What is a cover letter?

A cover letter is a professional-looking business letter, written with a personal touch, that is meant to "cover," or accompany, your résumé. You use a cover letter to tell an employer things like how and why you are a quick learner, friendly, helpful, and trustworthy, preferably by giving examples of when you showed these skills.

The good news is that your cover letter should be short. It will contain only three or four paragraphs and should not be more than one page long.

★ **TIP If you have little or no work experience, your cover letter can contain as few as two short paragraphs.**

Keep in mind that a cover letter is often your first introduction to an employer. First impressions count for a lot, so your cover letter must be a strong, sincere, honest, and clear statement about yourself, your intentions, and your abilities.

Why cover letters can make a difference

A cover letter is an important part of applying for almost any job. At a glance, it tells an employer . . .

- which job you want
- that you have the necessary skills and qualifications
- that you want to work for their company or organization
- how and where to contact you for an interview.

The job I'm applying for has an application form. Do I still have to write a cover letter?

No, it's not essential, but it's strongly advised. Going to the trouble of writing a cover letter may give you the edge over other candidates and get you an interview.

★ **TIP** **Make the best impression you can. Whenever you hand in an application form you should also attach your résumé and a cover letter.**

Do I need a cover letter when I'm applying for part-time or summer jobs?

Yes. It doesn't matter if you are applying for an entry-level full-time, part-time, or summer job, you will always need a cover letter.

I'm applying for so many jobs — can I re-use my cover letter?

No, that's not a great idea. Each job that you apply for will require a new, customized cover letter.

The good news is that once you have done one they get much easier and quicker to write. This is especially true if you are applying for several jobs of the same type. It's important to look carefully at the position you want and write your cover letter for that specific position. All jobs are different and require their own cover letters. Taking the time to write your letter for each job will help you get interviews.

LOOK AT IT FROM THE EMPLOYER'S POINT OF VIEW
An employer uses your cover letter as one more way to choose between you and other applicants. Many employers receive hundreds of applications and résumés. When there is a lot of competition for a job, a strong cover letter may be what sets you apart.

Who is it addressed to?

Before you begin, find out who you should send your application to and address your letter to that person. Use the person's name (make sure you've spelled it correctly) and title as given in the advertisement. If there is not a specific person listed, or if you are dropping off your résumé to an employer that has not specifically advertised a position, try to find out who will be doing the hiring. You can do this by phoning the employer first. Often the person who answers the phone can help you. It's easy. All you need to say is something like:

- "Hello. My name is __________ __________ . Could you tell me the name of the person in charge of hiring the summer staff?"

  or
- "Good morning. I'm applying for the part-time position that is posted in your window. Can you please tell me the name of the person I should address my application to?"

  or
- "Hello. I'm applying for the ____________________ position advertised in the newspaper yesterday. Could you please tell me who I should address my cover letter to?"

Be sure to ask for the correct spelling, and the person's title.

If you can't call to find out a name because the advertisement specifically requests "no phone calls, please," you will have to address your letter in general terms. For example, you can start your letter with "Dear Sir or Madam," "Dear Hiring Manager," or "Dear Selection Committee."

It's always best to have the correct person's name, so try to obtain it whenever possible. Going to the extra trouble always makes a good impression.

How do I set up my cover letter?

At the top of the letter, include your personal information:

- your name
- your address
- your phone number
- your e-mail address (if you have one, and you check it regularly)

Next, two lines down, comes the date. Then, two lines later, add the employer information:

- the hiring manager's name
- the hiring manager's title (e.g., Manager, Director of Human Resources, Owner)
- the full company name
- the company's address

Check out the samples on pages 61–64.

The three main parts of a cover letter

The opening

Remember, a cover letter should be short — no longer than one page — and will probably only contain only three or four paragraphs.

In the opening paragraph, state which position you are applying for (remember to quote a position number if the advertisement listed one) and where and when the position was advertised. If the job was not advertised in a newspaper or on a web site, be sure to say where and how you heard of the opening. Perhaps someone mentioned the position to you, or you saw a sign in a window, or picked up an application and information package at a job fair.

The middle

In the body of your letter, write one, two, or three short paragraphs that describe any of your skills, experience, or qualifications that directly relate to the position you are applying for. Mention the most important and most relevant items first. Don't repeat everything your résumé says. Just pick one or two specific experiences or achievements and relate them to the position you want.

If you haven't done this type of job before, or a similar type of job, it's okay to tell the employer. Let them know that you really want the job. Tell them you are a hard worker and give them an example of when you demonstrated this in another job, or at school, or on a sports team, or in a hobby. Explain to the employer that you are a quick learner and also give an example. List your personal strengths and qualities. Last, tell them that you'd really like to work for their company and say why.

The end

The closing paragraph should summarize why you are an excellent candidate and where you can be reached. Be clear, firm, and confident, but avoid overly emotional statements that seem needy or desperate.

What if I don't have any experience at all?

If this is your first job, or you do not feel you have enough experience that relates to the position, you're not alone. Everyone has doubts. But before you give up, take another look at your résumé. Re-read what is there and remind yourself of all the things you've done and all the things that make you a good and special person. What would your friends say about you? Now, think about the job you're applying for. Ask yourself: what qualities do I have that the employer will be looking for?

Another way to discover your relevant experience is to look closely at the advertisement or job posting. Often an ad tells you exactly what the employer wants to hear in a cover letter. Look for what comes after key phrases like: "The successful candidate will have . . ." or "If you are . . ."

Also, consider what it would be like to do the job. What qualities might the employer need in an employee? If you want to work in retail, where you have to handle cash and stock, then attributes like "honesty" and "trustworthiness" are important. So when you look back at your previous jobs, volunteer work, school activities, hobbies, sports, or extra-curricular activities, can you think of times when you demonstrated "honesty" or "trustworthiness"?

The trick is to match your own experiences, and the qualities they demonstrate in you, with what the employer will require of a successful candidate.

Here are some examples of the qualities employers tend to look for in an employee, matched up with common experiences:

EXPERIENCES	QUALITIES EMPLOYERS LOOK FOR
Sport	
played on a sporting team	team player, outgoing, motivated, driven
coached a kids team	a leader, reliable, trustworthy
Extra-curricular	
performed in a play	creative, able to speak in front of groups
play chess	able to concentrate, attentive to detail
play musical instruments	creative, dedicated, focused
At School	
strong at science	inquisitive, able to solve problems
strong at math	analytical, logical
strong at English	good at writing, communicating
strong at gym	physically strong, team player, dedicated
Volunteer Work	
helped at seniors home	sensitive, kind
worked with disabled	patient, caring
Previous Positions	
baby-sitter	trustworthy, flexible, calm, responsible
lifeguard	energetic, serious, independent

Match up your own experiences with the employer's needs. Put them in the body of your cover letter. Tell the employer you are capable of doing a great job because of your personal qualities. And always give supporting examples when you can.

How should it look? What style?

Your cover letter must be on either standard plain white, off-white, or very light grey 8 ½" x 11" paper. Always type your cover letter. If you don't have a computer, ask a friend if you can use theirs. Do not write it by hand. Use the same font style and size as your résumé. Single-space your cover letter, keeping a double space between paragraphs.

Be sure to spellcheck your letter, and have someone you trust read it over to make sure you don't have any spelling or grammar mistakes.

How should I send my cover letter?

If you are responding to an advertisement that states exactly how the employer wishes to receive your application, then always follow those instructions.

If it's left up to you, or you are responding to a "help wanted" sign or a lead from a friend, or you are taking initiative and simply forwarding your résumé, then follow these basic guidelines:

In person

For entry-level positions, it's always best to drop off your application in person. This way you'll be sure it arrives safely, and it gives you another opportunity to make a good impression. If it's possible, hand your application to the hiring manager personally. Remember to smile and dress neatly. You will also be able to see the company with your own eyes. Often you can pick up some information on the company at the reception desk. Read it carefully; it could be useful if you get an interview. You may feel intimidated or shy about just walking into a strange office. Everyone does — it's natural. But the more you do it, the easier it gets, and best of all, taking this kind of action will raise your confidence level and help you get that interview.

By fax

If an ad asks you to fax your application, then be sure to do a separate fax cover sheet. A fax cover sheet is like a title page. A typical one looks like this:

FAX COVER PAGE
From: Your name
Fax number: (416) 555-5555
Phone number: (416) 555-1234

Date: April 10, 2001

To: Mr. John Smith
Fax number: (416) 555-4444

Number of pages, including this cover: 4

Somewhere on the page (either at the very top or the very bottom) you should also include your address, your phone number, your fax number (if you have one), and your e-mail address.

By regular mail

If you are mailing in your application, use a large (9" x 12") envelope so you do not have to fold your résumé and cover letter. If your résumé is two pages long, staple the pages together. Attach your cover letter (and the application form, if there is one) to your résumé with a paper clip. Be sure to go to the post office and buy the correct postage for the envelope — it costs more to mail a large envelope than it does to mail a regular letter.

By e-mail

If you are asked to e-mail your application, make sure you know how to send an "attachment." If you're not sure how, have someone help you. It's a good idea to include your name and phone number in the "body" of your e-mail message so the employer will know how to contact you if your attachment doesn't work. This does occasionally happen. So, try to send a "simple" or "text-only" version of your attachment as well as your normal copy. This way, even if the employer is using older software and can't open the formatted version of your attachment, the basic information in your résumé and cover letter will still be clear.

Remember, sending a cover letter and résumé by e-mail shows that you know how to use your computer. But it will only impress an employer if you do it correctly. If you have any questions, ask a friend or teacher to help you.

DO'S AND DON'TS OF COVER LETTERS

✔
- *Do have an answering machine or voice mail hooked up to the phone number you provide in your letter.*
- *Do tell friends or family members to take detailed messages for you while you are job searching.*
- *Do use an e-mail address that is proper (avoid nicknames or slang) and be sure you check your e-mail often during your job search.*
- *Do have someone you trust (teacher, parent, friend, employment counsellor) proofread your cover letter. Poor grammar and spelling mistakes are unprofessional. Take the extra time to ensure they are avoided. Write a new cover letter for every job you apply for.*

✗
- *Don't say how much you want to be paid in your cover letter, unless an advertisement asks you to give a salary expectation.*
- *Don't put your references in your cover letter.*
- *Don't rush your letter. After you've written it, wait a day, then look at it again with a fresh perspective.*
- *Don't forget to sign your letter in blue or black pen.*
- *Don't oversell yourself. It's important to be confident, but don't overdo it.*

Checklist — The Cover Letter:

- My phone number is on my cover letter.
- I have an answering machine hooked up to the phone number I'm using and the outgoing message is straightforward and professional.
- I have the correct spelling of the hiring manager's name.
- If there is a position number or title, I have quoted it in my letter.
- In the body of my letter, I have included my most relevant experience first.
- I have said some positive things about myself that relate to the job.
- I have spellchecked my letter and had someone I trust read it over for errors.
- I have signed my letter.

Sample cover letters

To get you started, on pages 61 to 64 are four examples of great cover letters for first jobs. You can follow them as examples, but don't just copy them. Be yourself. There is no "perfect" or "right" cover letter because everyone is different. Make your cover letters reflect who you are, what you can do and offer, and what you enjoy.

- See page 61 for an example of a cover letter for a job similar to one the applicant has had before. (Applicant: Jacob Poulos)

- See page 62 for an example of a cover letter for when the applicant has relevant experience, but it's not an exact match for the position. (Applicant: Emma Cho)

- See page 63 for a cover letter for a situation in which the applicant's experience is not related to the job being applied for. (Applicant: Mohammed Akil)

- See page 64 for a great sample cover letter for when the applicant has no *direct* experience but the experience they do have is indirectly related to the job being applied for. (Applicant: Jesse Brown)

I still need more help with my cover letter . . .

Cover letters can sometimes be difficult to write, especially if it's your first time. Lots of people can help you. Just remember, among your parents, teachers, friends, and siblings you will be able to find someone who has written a cover letter at some point in their life. Ask them to give you a hand. Also, there are many places to go to get cover letter help from professionals — and most services for youth are free. Check out chapter 10 of this book for help in finding a centre near you.

JACOB POULOS
12 King Street,
Victoria, BC V1W 1A1
(250) 555-3333
jacobp@internet.com

April 10, 2001

Ms. Jennifer Burton
Day Camp Director
Camp Wannabe
222 Lions Bridge Rd.,
Suite 201,
Victoria, BC V2R 3Y2

Dear Ms. Burton:

RE: Junior Day Camp Counsellor

I wish to apply for the position of Junior Day Camp Counsellor at Camp Wannabe as advertised on a flyer in the guidance office at my high school.

I love summer camp. Until last year, I spent a month of every summer as a camper at Camp Lotsafun, a residential camp for kids. Over my years there I learned over 100 camp songs. During my last summer as a Counsellor in Training, I learned how to set an example for the younger campers and to be a positive role model. I was often responsible for planning and leading games and crafts activities. Being a leader was a great learning opportunity for me. I developed a strong sense of responsibility — something every counsellor needs.

As you can see from my attached résumé, I will be finishing grade 10 in June and would be available to work all summer, full-time. I think I would make an excellent day camp counsellor and I look forward to hearing from you about an interview.
My telephone number is (250) 555-3333.

Sincerely,

Jacob Poulos

Jacob Poulos

EMMA CHO

4667–413 22nd Ave.,
Edmonton, AB T6K 1Z2
(403) 555-7890
Emma@theweb.ca

January 10, 2001

Dr. Eva Night
2 South St.,
Edmonton, AB T5L 4A3

Dear Dr. Night:

At my friend Scott Smith's last appointment, you mentioned that you would be needing some extra reception help in your office soon. He was kind enough to pass this information on to me. If this is still the case, I would like to offer my services.

For the past three months I have been working part-time, three evenings per week, as a telemarketer at ABC Corp., downtown. Talking with up to fifty customers per evening, I have gained a great deal of customer service experience. I am confident on the phone and I also have basic computer skills.

Attached is my résumé. I would be available to work part-time weekdays. I have always thought of doctors' offices as friendly environments and so I know I would enjoy working with you. I hope to hear from you soon.

Sincerely,

Emma Cho

Emma Cho

MOHAMMED AKIL

345 Dunberry Lane,
Toronto, ON M5E 2I7
(416) 555-6178

April 11, 2000

Andrea Klauss
Manager, Downtown Cinemas
2789 Main Street
Toronto, ON M8R 2K5

Dear Andrea Klauss,

Please accept my résumé as application for the Downtown Cinemas Box Office Attendant position advertised by the Help Wanted sign you have posted. I am very excited about possibly joining your team.

As someone who goes to see movies all the time, I know what it takes to be a good box office attendant. I am polite and friendly and I know I would be a good representative for Downtown Cinemas. From my experience playing on many different sports teams at my school, I know I will get along well with my co-workers, and can always be relied upon to help out when I'm needed. Please call me at my home number, (416) 555-6178, to arrange a time when I can come in and speak with you. My family or voice mail will take a message for me if I am not in. I go to school from Monday to Friday between 9:00 a.m. and 3:45 p.m. but I would be free any other time. Thank you for your consideration.

Sincerely,

Mohammed Akil

Mohammed Akil

JESSE BROWN

36 Custer St.,
Vancouver, BC V6K 2K8
Tel: (604) 555-1175

May 22, 2000

Felix Katz
Manager, CD Emporium
420 McDonald Ave., Suite 102
Vancouver, BC V3T 5K7

Dear Mr. Katz,

I came into the store yesterday and spoke to Josh, who suggested that if I was interested in submitting my résumé, you would keep it on file. I would like to be considered for any position that becomes available.

I have been to your store many times and it seems like a really great place to work. I am hardworking and responsible and I get along well with people. I know you probably prefer to hire people with retail experience, but in my case I think you should make an exception.

As you can see on my résumé, I love music. I love to play music, listen to music, and someday I would like to write music. I am so enthusiastic about all types of music that I know I would be a great person to help people buy CDs. I realize I would have a lot to learn, but I also feel I already have a lot to offer.

I would love a chance to come in to talk to you in person. I will call you Friday afternoon to arrange a time for us to meet. If it is easier for you, please feel free to contact me at my home number, (604) 555-1175. Thank you for your time.

Sincerely,

Jesse Brown

6

Job Searching

"Where are all the jobs?"

Did you know that many jobs, especially entry-level jobs, are never advertised in newspapers? This surprises most people. How, you might ask, can I find out about a job if it's not advertised somewhere? This chapter will help you discover all the different ways you can find out about positions that are available, and give you advice on how to apply for them. Job searching takes time and effort, but if you stick with it, you will succeed.

What's the very first thing I should do?

Before you do anything else, it's a great idea to tell everyone you know that you are looking for a job. Tell them to tell people they know. This is called networking.

How can I network?

Networking is an excellent way to let job leads come to you. It will be more important to your chances of getting a job than anything else you do.

Take a few hours and call everyone you can think of and say something like this:

- "Hi, it's (your name). I just wanted to give you a quick call. I'm looking for a (summer/part-time/full-time) job. So I'm calling everyone I can to let them know I'm looking. I'm interested in (types of jobs). If you hear of anything at all can you let me know? I'd really appreciate any help you can give me. Thanks very much."

FACT **Many young people get their first few jobs through connections. Parents, teachers, siblings, friends, parents of friends, aunts and uncles, neighbours, and coaches are all excellent sources of information about job openings.**

It's important to tell people what kind of job you are looking for and what special skills you have to offer. Remember, networking is not asking for a job. Networking is making connections with people you already know and asking them to keep their eye out for suitable positions for you. The more people you tell, the better your chances will be.

Does networking work?

Try this: think about how fast rumours spread. Now imagine if you could use this for good, to help you get a job! That's kind of what networking does. It uses the power of association to help you get what you want: a job. Remember to thank people for "keeping their eye out for a job for you," and now that you are a part of their network, be prepared for them to ask you to return the favour sometime.

What if "networking" just isn't done in my culture?

There's no need to feel shy or ashamed about asking friends and family to keep you in mind as they hear about jobs. In some cultures, of course, networking isn't done. But in Canada networking is very common and people do it when they're looking for all kinds of things like an apartment, a used car, a good restaurant or music store, even a new dentist. Make sure you explain this to any friends or family who are newer to Canada and don't understand why you are asking them to help you look for a job.

TRUE STORIES

Being in the Right Place at the Right Time

- **Anna heard about her job from her sister, Jennie. Jennie was speaking with her boyfriend's mother, Carol. At Carol's shop they needed a part-time person right away because someone had just quit and it was getting close to Christmas. Later, Jennie told this to Anna, and Anna called Carol. Anna had an interview the next day. She got the job right away.**
- **Troy's uncle Gus works in a factory. Gus heard from his boss Peta that the front office would soon be hiring for an entry-level position. Did he know a young person who was looking for a job? No, he said. Then, luckily, Troy called Gus to tell him he was looking for a job. "Well, you've got great timing, young man," said Gus. "I think we're hiring. Call me at work tomorrow. I'll put you through to the boss, Peta." Troy got the job the next week.**

★ **TIP** Remember to thank the person who helps you find a job. You never know when you might need their help again. Everyone likes to be appreciated.

Where should I start looking?

After you have begun to network with as many people as you can think of, it's time to try the other routes.

★ **TIP Act on a good lead right away. The sooner you make that phone call, the greater the chances that you'll be ahead of someone else.**

Classifieds: how to read job ads

In most newspapers, the classified section is still a good source of job openings. This is especially true if you are looking for full-time or part-time work. Generally speaking, classifieds are not as good for summer jobs, although many do carry some summer jobs or "seasonal" postings during the summer months.

Looking in the classifieds takes patience. In big cities, there may be as many as five newspapers to look through. Be sure to check out the major daily papers, as well as the free weekly newspapers, as these also have job listings. You will soon get to know which papers in your area carry the kinds of jobs you are looking for and on which days they run. This makes it easier and less time-consuming.

Keep in mind how many other people also look through the classifieds. You've got a lot of competition, so don't let it be the only way you look for jobs.

Classified tips

- Always circle an interesting ad when you see it and keep going. Come back to the circled ones at the end.
- Look through the ads in the morning. Sometimes jobs fill quickly and the afternoon might be too late.

- Most libraries and employment centres have free newspapers for you to look through.
- Read the ad you're interested in many times. Make sure you have the skills and qualifications they are looking for.

Spotting classified "scams"

Be very wary of classified ads that sound too good to be true. If an ad promises to pay you beyond your wildest dreams and says "no experience necessary," or "Hey Students! Make $1,000 per week," it means there is probably a catch, and it might be a scam.

★ **TIP Scam warning** **Never pay an employer your own money before you start a job. You should not have to pay for the products you are going to sell. Don't sign a sales contract without having someone you trust, like a parent, teacher, or friend, review it first.**

Why are there so many sales ads in the classified section?

Many young people work in sales jobs, whether that means working in a retail shop, telemarketing, or selling things door to door. Sales jobs can be very exciting and fast-paced, and will often pay quite well, especially if you are good at selling. But beware! One of the reasons there seem to be so many sales jobs advertised is because selling can be really tough, and the way you get paid (for example, by commission) is often not very secure or reliable. So before you accept a job offer, make sure you know what's involved. For more about sales jobs, commissions, and base pay, see pages 111–12.

★ **TIP It's easier to sell something that you yourself believe in, use, or think is a good product or service.**

What is the "hidden job market"?

The "hidden job market" is a term that refers to the many jobs that are never advertised in the newspapers. Companies and organizations, especially smaller ones, often rely on internal postings and word of mouth to attract potential candidates.

How do I tap into the hidden job market?

Here are some of the ways you can reach jobs in the hidden job market:

- networking
- applying in person to discover unadvertised jobs
- seeking out free employment programs and services
- searching on the Internet
- attending job fairs and visiting job banks
- conducting information interviews
- self-advertising
- cold calling

Applying in person

A common and successful way to look for a job is by applying in person. In fact, for some industries, such as retail and restaurants, employers often prefer that you apply in person. When you go, have a stack of résumés with you, but be prepared to pick up an application form (see chapter 3) too. (And remember to follow the Ten Steps to a Successful Application Form listed on pages 25–27.)

Free programs and services

Many communities in Canada have employment services specifically geared toward youth. Read chapter 10 to see how you can find such a service in your own town or city, or contact your province's ministry of labour by visiting their web site or looking them up in the government listings (the "blue pages") of the phone book. You can also try looking up "employment" in your local phone book or Yellow Pages.

The main benefit of *youth* employment centres is that, compared with other employment agencies, they are specially equipped to help young people find jobs. Many also have access to jobs that are not advertised elsewhere and are reserved especially for young people. It's definitely worth giving one a call.

Internet searches and finding jobs online

The Internet is a great place to look for job postings, so if you can, get online. These days most jobs are posted somewhere on the web, either on private sites, government sites, or in the online version of the newspaper classifieds. In the back of this book you will find some good web sites to get you started.

The web is also a good place to learn about the company you're applying to. In its web site, a company or organization will usually give you a summary of the products and services it offers, as well as a listing of the people who work there. It can be a great place to gather information for writing a cover letter, or to prepare for an interview.

What if I don't have a computer at home?

If you don't have a computer at home, or if it's not fast enough to do good Internet searches, you can get access from other places, such as libraries, employment centres, a friend's house, or a school or college computer lab.

★ **TIP** Many jobs are "advertised" when friends send leads or postings to each other via e-mail. Instead of paying for ad space in a newspaper, some companies send out job openings to their employees and ask them to forward the notices to anyone they know who might be qualified. This is another reason why developing a strong network is becoming so important. Phone or e-mail everyone you know and tell them you are looking for a job.

What if I'm moving? How can I look for a job in another city or province?

The Internet has made it easy to look for a job in another part of Canada. If you are moving, or you're spending your summer somewhere else, you can search for jobs in Toronto from Halifax. You can send in your résumé for a job in Ottawa from Whitehorse. Job searching is getting much easier with the Internet.

Job fairs

At job fairs, a number of employers who are hiring come together and set up booths to talk directly to job searchers. They are often held in halls, schools, malls, hotels, conference centres, arenas, or employment centres. They are a great way to meet potential employers face to face, fill out applications, submit your résumé, and learn about different companies and organizations. Sometimes they even have on-the-spot interviews — so be prepared. When you go, look your best and be sure to bring along copies of your résumé so you can take full advantage of the event.

★ **TIP** **Remember to dress neatly and be very polite when you attend a job fair. Make a good impression on potential employers. Also, keep track of the names of the employers to whom you've handed in your résumés. Take every opportunity to talk with employers. The more practice you get, the easier you will find interviews.**

Job banks

Job banks are listings, created by either governments or private companies, of current positions available by region. You can access most job banks on the Internet. It takes time to go through them, but they are a very important resource for job searchers.

If you need help with the Internet, whether to do searches or to send your résumé via e-mail, ask a friend, librarian, teacher, or relative, or call your local youth employment centre.

What's an internal posting?

A position is "posted internally" when it is advertised only within the company that is doing the hiring. This might mean the job is posted on the company bulletin board or sent around as an e-mail message. In some cases employers will simply tell their employees that a position is available and ask them to encourage anyone they know might be qualified to call for more information. Companies and organizations save money on advertising this way. They also benefit because the candidates often come recommended by someone already on staff.

The only way to hear about internal postings is to network. You never know who may help you. Tell as many people as you can that you are looking for a job so someone will think of you when an internal posting becomes available.

Information interviews

A great way to introduce yourself to an employer is to ask for an information interview. This is becoming a very common tool for young people, especially those who are trying to break into a specific field of interest.

If you have your sights set on a particular career, industry, or field and you need to learn more about it, then one way is to call or e-mail someone who already works in that field and ask for an information interview. Ask around. See if your parents, friends, or other acquaintances know someone in the field you are interested in. They may be able to help you set up an information interview. It may be that you'll need to make a "cold call" to someone who doesn't know you. See pages 78–81 for more information and tips on how to make these kinds of calls.

When it comes time to conduct an information interview, it is important to be well prepared. You should have a list of questions written out and take notes. Keep your questions short, as the person's time is valuable, and even though you are not applying for a job right now, you might one day meet again. So, it's important that you leave the person with a good impression.

Information interviews offer an opportunity for you to learn about what it takes to break into your field of interest. Here are some of the things you should ask about:

What are the typical educational requirements?
Where do most people obtain these qualifications?
What does a typical day look like for the person you're interviewing? What would they recommend you do to get into the field?
How did they break into the field?
What other tips can the person give you?
Could the person recommend anyone else you should talk to?

Are there any good books or articles that you should read to research the field?

Someone who already works in a field that you wish to enter can be a great contact in years to come. You never know how, or when, that person may help you. Be polite, enthusiastic, and very thankful for their time.

Internships and co-op placements

Many organizations and companies work hand in hand with schools, colleges, and universities to provide internship and co-op positions. These are full-time or part-time positions that typically last for a few months of the year and add to your classroom learning by giving you on-the-job experience and school credits. Although they don't pay much, and sometimes nothing at all, they are an excellent way to learn about an industry, make contacts, and ultimately land a job. Companies do tend to hire interns or co-op students over other applicants because they already know the company and how it works — and they've already proven themselves to be good workers and right for the position.

In some industries, especially media-based ones, an internship is fast becoming the only way to break into the industry. Almost no entry-level jobs are advertised in the arts industries like film, TV, publishing, newspaper, graphic design, and multi-media industries, as they are always filled by co-op students and interns. To find out more about how you can become an intern or co-op student, call your local community college or set up an information interview with someone in the field.

Volunteering

One of the best ways to gain valuable on-the-job experience is to volunteer for a non-profit organization, a charity, or a person you know who is in need. You'll be doing good in your community.

This, more than anything else, is what employers like to see in a potential employee. Someone who cares about others is the kind of person most employers want to hire.

Although you won't get paid to volunteer, the experience you'll gain is also a great reason to volunteer, especially if you haven't worked before, or you don't have a lot of work experience. A volunteer position is a great addition to your résumé. Like a paying job, it tells an employer that you made a commitment, stuck it out, and were successful. The person who supervised you at your volunteer job is also a good person to obtain a reference from.

FACT **You might be thinking that volunteering is like working for nothing. It's not. Volunteering is a great way to meet people, learn on-the-job skills, and network. Many people get jobs while they are volunteering because they are in the right place at the right time.**

Treat volunteering like a real job. Be reliable, prompt, and friendly. When you show this attitude, the people you are working with will want you to succeed. And they will want to help you get a paid job.

Getting a volunteer job takes time and a little effort. There may be a volunteer centre in your community that can help you. Check out your local phone book or www.volunteer.ca for a centre near you.

Apprenticeships

A growing number of young Canadians are exploring the option of doing an apprenticeship. This is a great way to learn the skills needed to enter a skilled trade — and to earn money while you do it. Talk to your guidance counsellor if you are at school, an employment counsellor, or call your province's ministry in charge of training. There are well over one hundred different trades that offer apprenticeships and let you earn while you learn. After you've finished being trained, many of these jobs are very well paid. There are hundreds of career options to discover.

Self-advertising

One way of getting employment is to advertise yourself. This is especially effective if you are offering a service such as baby-sitting, lawn mowing, raking leaves, designing web sites, house painting, or doing odd jobs. There are many inexpensive ways to advertise yourself, from posting flyers and placing ads in your local papers, to making direct contact by phone, fax, or e-mail.

★ **TIP Remember your own personal safety. If you are going out on a job, make sure you tell someone the address and phone number of where you are going.**

Self-employment

A fast-growing sector of employment for young people is self-employment. Self-employment means becoming your own boss and starting up a small business. This is not an option for everyone, as there are many challenges to face, but if you have a real drive to become an entrepreneur, nothing will stand in your way. To find out more about the self-employment option, call an employment centre near you, a business centre, or your local Human Resources Centre of Canada and ask about the resources available to you in your province.

Cold calling

Cold calling simply means picking up the phone and calling someone you don't know to gather information for your job search.

Cold calling is a great way to . . .

- get information about possible job leads
- introduce yourself to a potential employer and tell them about your skills and interests
- find out if an employer is hiring soon
- set up an information interview
- gain the kind of confidence you'll need to succeed in an interview.

Yes, in the beginning it takes a while to get up the nerve to make a cold call. While some people don't mind just calling someone out of the blue, for others it takes a while to gain the confidence. But once you've done it a few times, you'll find it's easy. It's just talking on the phone, right? You do that all the time.

How do I find out who to call, and how do I get their phone number?

There are many ways to find the names and phone numbers of potential employers:

- Check out your local phone book or Yellow Pages if you know what kinds of employers or places you're looking for.
- Some employment books are also good sources of information on companies. For example, *The Canada Student Employment Guide*, which is published each year, lists which companies across Canada hire students and tells you what they look for.
- Business directories are big books that list businesses by

location, product, or service. You can find them in your local Human Resources Centre of Canada, employment resource centre, or library.
- The Internet is a great source of company information. A company's web site will give you a phone number, and will often give you the name of the person in charge of human resources, or of the sector of the company you are interested in learning about. Do a search.
- The newspaper is an often-overlooked resource. Pay attention to articles on employers who look like they might be expanding. Look up their numbers and give them a call. A good way to start the conversation is to say you saw the piece in the paper.

So, what should I say?

When you're cold calling, the best approach is to take some time and decide what you want to say before you call. Remember, what you want is information. Don't put the employer on the spot by asking them for a job right away. But if the conversation goes well, don't be afraid to politely ask if, or when, there will be any openings.

Write down what you want to say, and some questions to ask. This is especially helpful if you get the person's voice mail. Remember to . . .

- speak clearly
- be very polite
- if someone referred you to that person, start off the conversation by telling them who gave you their name
- ask if you could have a few minutes of their time
- give your name and why you are calling first
- be prepared to talk about your interests and skills
- if the call goes well, ask if there are any suitable positions available either now or in the future.

Here are some examples of things to say:

To start things off:

- "Hi, my name is __________ __________ . I'm in my last semester as a student at Eastside High, and now I'm looking for a full-time position so I'm gathering some information for my job search. I wonder if you could help me out for a few moments?"
- "Good morning, Mr. Smith. My name is __________ __________ . I'm currently job searching and I'm researching companies in the ______________ sector. I was looking at your web site yesterday and I had a few questions about your company. I wonder if you have a few minutes to give me some more information?"
- "Hi, it's __________ __________ calling. Jim Lobe suggested I give you a call. I'm gathering some information because I'm job searching at the moment and Jim thought you'd be a good person to talk to. You see, I'm very interested in companies like yours because ___________________________ ."

★ **TIP** **Smile on the phone. It will affect how you are heard. And be enthusiastic — it's infectious. People do like helping other people, so give them every reason to think that if they help you, you'll make them feel good by thanking them. Who knows, they might need a favour from you one day.**

If you are seriously looking for a job, and not just gathering information for your job search, don't be afraid to come right out and ask the employer if there are any positions available. If the conversation seems to be going well, say something like:

- "I was wondering if you expect to be doing any hiring soon?"
- "May I send along my résumé for you to keep on file in case any positions come up in the near future?"

Remember, if you don't ask, you'll never know. The worst they can say is: "No, not at the moment" or "I'm not sure, I'd have to ask around." So, there is nothing to be afraid of. They might say: "As a matter of fact, we do have an opening coming up soon. Why don't you send me your résumé?"

DO'S AND DON'TS OF JOB SEARCHING

✔

- ***Do tell everyone you know that you are job searching. Develop a network.***
- ***Do look through the newspaper classified ads in the morning. Sometimes jobs fill quickly and the afternoon might be too late.***
- ***Do take an application home and fill it out neatly and carefully.***
- ***Do dress neatly when you go to job fairs and drop off résumés.***
- ***Do be enthusiastic when you are cold calling.***

✘

- ***Don't go unprepared to an information interview. Take the time to learn about the company and prepare some questions.***
- ***Don't wait until you move. Look for a job on the Internet before you get there.***
- ***Don't feel you have to accept a job if you sense that it's a scam.***
- ***Don't ever pay an employer your own money before you start a job.***

Where to get more job-searching help . . .

Knowing how and where to look for a job can be difficult when you're starting out. Almost everyone, at some time in their life, has been where you are and knows how difficult it can be. Ask around for some advice. Try a teacher, guidance counsellor, family member, or youth worker. Also, keep in mind that there are professionals at youth employment centres who can help you look for work. Many of these places also list actual jobs and most services are completely free. Check out chapter 10 for help in finding a centre near you.

7

Before an Interview

"How do I prepare for an interview?"

Always keep a positive attitude when you're job searching. You should be prepared to get a call from an employer asking you in for an interview at any time. It's a good idea to keep your résumé, paper, and a pen beside the phone at all times. That way you'll be ready when the phone rings.

Because it's likely that you'll be applying for several jobs at once, be prepared to respond. When you get a call, don't say, "Which one was that again?" Know the jobs you've applied for. Keep a list by the phone.

Make sure you check your answering machine frequently if you are out. If an employer calls, return the call as soon as you can. But remember to take a few moments to decide what you're going to say. Have your résumé, pen, and paper handy.

★ **TIP** **Make sure you have a working answering machine or voice mail hooked up to your phone in case you're not home when an employer calls. Tell the people you live with how important it is that you get detailed messages.**

What will an employer say when they call me in for an interview?

Here is what the conversation might sound like when an employer calls a young job searcher to set up an interview:

— "Hi, it's John Smith from Noble Company. I've read your résumé and cover letter and I'm calling to find out if you're still interested in applying for the position."
— "Yes, very much."
— "Great. Then I'd like to set up a time for you to come in for an interview. Do you have a pen and paper?"
— "Yes, I do."
— "Okay, we're doing the interviews at the end of the week. How does Friday morning at 10:30 sound?"
— "That's fine for me."
— "Do you know where we are located?"
— "Yes, I know the address, but what's the fastest way there by bus?"
— "Take the number 4 bus from downtown. It comes right past the front door."
— "Thanks. May I take down your phone number and extension in case I need to reach you?"
— "Yes, it's 555-5555, extension 234."
— "Got it, great. Okay, Mr. Smith, I'll see you on Friday morning at 10:30. I'm glad you called and I'm looking forward to meeting you."

★ **TIP** **Confirm the time and day of the interview at the end of the conversation, just to be sure you've heard correctly and finish the call with a firm "thank you."**

What else should I ask when an employer calls?

In the example above, the candidate asked for clear directions. If you've never been to the place in person, this is a very good question. It'll give you a chance to learn exactly where the company is located and how long it'll take you to get there for your interview. If you honestly don't know the answers, here are some other good questions to ask when an employer calls you in for an interview:

- "Can you confirm the address for me?"
- "Do you have a web site I could look at to learn more about the company before the interview?"
- "May I stop by your office and pick up some information on your organization before the interview?"

The employer is listening carefully to how you conduct yourself from the very beginning. Try to be as polite, eager, and confident as you can, even on the first call. It is their first impression of you and you want to make it a good one.

★ **TIP This first conversation, when an employer calls to ask you in for an interview, is not the time ask, "What does the job pay?" The employer will bring up salary or wages if you have a successful interview.**

How do I research the company or organization?

It is a very good strategy to research the company or organization to prepare for your interview. Check out the company's web site and read all the company history, goals, objectives, mission statements, and frequently asked questions (FAQs). Go to the company and ask the receptionist for their annual report or other company literature. Go to the library and learn more about the industry in general. Search the library for newspaper articles and business directories. Network with people in the same industry to learn more about the company.

If the company manufactures a product, try to find out what it does and where it's sold. If they deliver a service, find out who are their typical clients and who benefits from their service. If you have an interview for a job in a restaurant, try to eat there so you know what's on the menu and the kind of place it is. If the job is in a shop, think about the kind of things they sell and the kind of customers they will usually get. The more you know going into an interview, the better you will look to an employer and the more confident you will feel.

How do I research the position?

Some positions are common to many organizations and they will be fairly similar wherever you work. If you've never held a similar position before, then it is important to learn as much about the type of job and its duties as you can. If you know anyone who does a similar job, ask them about it. What do they do in a typical day? What tasks are most important to their employer? This will give you a sense of the kind of skills the employer will be looking for in the interview and you will be better prepared to highlight your own skills in those areas.

★ **TIP Get to the interview a little early and ask if there is any information on the company for you to read.**

What should I do the night before an interview?

You might be a little nervous the night before the interview, but it's important to get a good night's sleep. You'll want to be fresh and wide awake during the interview.

If your interview is in the morning, make sure you set your alarm clock. It is very important that you are not late for an interview, as it makes a very poor first impression.

What should I wear to an interview?

Dress nicely. A good rule of thumb is to imagine that you got the job, and picture what you would wear on a typical day. Then, for the interview, dress a little more formally than you would if you were at work there. Job interviews call for your smartest-looking clothes.

Make sure your clothes are clean, and pressed if they require it. If you feel you don't have the right clothes, try to borrow them for the interview. Ask a friend who is the same size as you. Don't worry about overdressing; they are expecting you to try and impress them. And remember, all the other candidates will be well dressed.

Also, make sure you are clean and well groomed. The effort you put in to looking your best will always be to your advantage.

What should I bring with me to the interview?

Here is a list of things you should bring with you to the interview:

- the exact address, including: suite number, floor, office number, wing, or any other specific directions you were given.
- the name of the person who will be interviewing you.
- the phone number of the company and the extension of the person you're meeting so you can call them in the unlikely event you are running late.
- a separate list of references, typed neatly on a separate sheet. This is important, even if you've already given them to the employer on an application form. A separate sheet shows you are organized and are thinking ahead.

- two extra clean copies of your résumé — one for you to look at during the interview and an extra one for the employer, just in case they've misplaced theirs or they only have a blurry faxed copy.
- three possible prepared questions for the end of the interview (see pages 92–93 for help).
- a notepad or paper, so that you can take notes. Always ask permission to take notes in an interview.

What are references?

A reference is someone who agrees to speak to a potential employer about you and your abilities in a positive way. See pages 15–17 in chapter 2 for more information about how to choose your references, and what to ask them.

Don't wait until the last minute to get together your references. Be prepared as early as possible and always ask them for permission first.

Should I practise my interview skills?

Yes. Ask someone you trust to help you with your interview skills. Ask them to interview you as a "rehearsal."

Think success and it will happen . . .

During the interview you are likely going to be in a room, sitting in a chair, talking with an employer (or two) across a desk. Imagine yourself sitting up straight, head held high, answering the questions confidently. You should be able to talk easily about what you've done in the past and what you enjoy.

★ **TIP** It's okay if you're nervous. If you forget what you were going to say, admit you are nervous and move on. Being nervous is normal. It happens to everyone.

✓ **Three things to keep in mind**

1. Know what's on your résumé.
2. Answer every question in full. Say more than "Yes" or "No." Give an example from a previous job, hobby, or school experience that illustrates your answer.
3. Sell yourself. Be confident. You will get the job.

What are some common topics I will be asked about?

Be prepared to answer questions related to these topics:

- your previous work experience
- your skills and qualifications
- your preferred work environment
- your education
- your attitude toward the position you're applying for
- your extra-curricular interests, hobbies, and values
- why you want the job
- your availability

What are some tricky questions I can prepare for?

Q: What are your expectations of this job? Why do you want the job?

For a question like this state how you want to do a great job, learn lots, and make a good contribution to the company.

Q: What did you not like about your previous job?

First, try to say that this is a tough question because you did like your last job. Be specific and state something that you were very successful at, or had a good influence on. Then, pick something you honestly felt wasn't great at your last job, but don't dwell on it. Move on quickly.

Never, never, never say bad things about your previous employer, even if you left on bad terms and you feel you were completely in the right. Employers almost always respond badly to this because they identify with the employer. Make sure you have thought of at least one good thing to say about your previous position. You can't lie about the reason you left a previous job, especially if you were fired, but you can say you've learned a great deal from the experience you had at your last job and would be able to bring that knowledge to this new position.

Q: How long do you intend to be with the company?

If you are applying for a part-time or full-time position, then try not to commit yourself to a specific amount of time. You can simply say that you look forward to being a part of the team and growing with the job. If they press you for an answer it's better to say a longer period of time than a shorter period. Two years is generally appropriate because employers don't like fast turnover, as it takes time to train new people.

Q: Tell me about yourself.

Because this is such a broad request, some people don't know what to say. Give a general overview of education, work experience, and where you're at now. Keep your comments work-related. Stay focused. Be brief. This question is often used to see how well someone can focus and organize their thoughts. Don't ramble on about your childhood.

Q: Where do you see yourself in five years?

This is a good time to be honest. If you've got a long-term goal to go back to school or to do something that you've always dreamed of, then say it. Five years is a long way off, especially for a young person. Showing an employer that you've got dreams and goals is very important. Make sure, however, that your goals sound sufficiently far off that the employer doesn't think you'll want to leave too soon to pursue them. Try to cast the job as a step to realizing your dreams. Perhaps it's an important learning experience for you, or a great way to earn and save some money.

If you are trying to break into a specific field, and the job you're applying for is a career move, then this question is a great opportunity for you to really tell an employer about your goals. Don't be unrealistic or aggressive, just be honest and enthusiastic.

Q: Tell me something about yourself that you want to change. (Or, What is your greatest weakness?)

This is possibly the most common tricky question. Everyone hates it because it really puts you on the spot. The way around it is to come up with a negative quality that is not directly related to the job you're applying for, or to admit to a weakness that you're actively improving. *Whatever you do, have an answer prepared just in case you're asked this question.* After all, everyone has weaknesses and it doesn't look good if you think you have none. Even if you acknowledge that it's a tough question, it's always best to answer rather than not.

There are still good and bad answers to this question. For example, it's better to admit to being "a little competitive at times," or to say, "My best friend says I can be opinionated," than it is to say, "I have trouble getting out of bed in the morning" or "I didn't get along with my last boss." Try to decide on something that's right for you. Make sure you let the employer know how you're taking steps to change the behaviour.

★ **TIP** Talk yourself up. Always speak enthusiastically about your experiences. If you have to mention something negative, try to see the good in it. Talk about what you've learned. Give negative experiences a "positive spin." Don't be embarrassed to talk about yourself in a positive light. You don't have to brag — just be confident and only talk about your strengths. An interview is not a time to be shy!

What questions should I ask an employer at the end of an interview?

Many interviews conclude with the employer saying something like this: "I think that's it from me. Do you have any questions?"

Be prepared for this. Take time before the interview to prepare a list of questions. Get out your sheet and take a moment to read them over. Make sure the employer has covered everything on your list. Often, most things will have been covered but it's important to make sure you've learned everything you can about the position.

Even if everything seems to have been covered, it's still good to ask a question or two. Here is a list of some good questions for the end of an interview:

- "If I'm successful, what kind of training would I receive?"
- "Could you tell me the next step in the hiring process?"
- "If I'm successful, who would I report to?"
- "When would the position start?"

✔ **Checklist — Before the Interview**

Make sure you have . . .

- **a short list of questions to ask the employer**
- **two fresh copies of your résumé**
- **a separate sheet with your references' names, addresses, phone numbers, titles, and relationship to you, typed neatly and in full (see pages 14–17 for more information on references)**
- **your interview clothes laid out and shoes cleaned**
- **the directions to the interview, a ride there or bus fare, and an understanding of how long it will take**
- **the company's phone number, in case you get lost or held up.**

DO'S AND DON'TS OF INTERVIEW PREPARATION

✔
- *Do treat the initial phone call as the first stage of the interview.*
- *Do be on time.*
- *Do bring copies of your résumé.*
- *Do bring a typed list of references.*
- *Do smile.*
- *Do be polite.*
- *Do give examples.*
- *Do bring the address, phone number, and name of the person interviewing you, so you can call just in case you get lost or delayed.*
- *Do be enthusiastic and have a positive attitude.*
- *Do make eye contact and shake the interviewer's hand firmly.*
- *Do dress nicely — a little better than the job itself would require.*
- *Do thank the interviewer for their time.*
- *Do ask what the next step will be after the interview.*
- *Do give examples of accomplishments.*

✘
- *Don't lie.*
- *Don't talk too much but don't give one-word answers either.*
- *Don't talk negatively about previous employers.*
- *Don't chew gum.*
- *Don't smoke right before going in — it will smell and might give a bad impression.*
- *Don't be rude to anyone you meet on your way in.*
- *Don't slouch in your seat.*
- *Don't fidget with pen, hair, etc.*

I still need more help to prepare for my interview . . .

Interviews can sometimes be difficult to prepare for, especially if it's your first time. Lots of people can help you. Just remember, among your parents, teachers, friends, and siblings you will be able to find someone who has either been through or given an interview at some point in their lives. Ask them to give you a hand. Also, there are lots of places to go to get interview help from professionals. Most services for youth are free. Check out chapter 10 for help in finding a centre near you.

8

All About Interviews

"What do I need to know?"

Now we know that the most important part of having a successful interview is to be prepared. Next you are going to find out about the different kinds of interviews, what to expect during the interview, and what to do after it's all over.

What is the employer looking for?

The employer is looking for the right person for the job, and you want them to believe that it's you! So think of an interview as a conversation. You're not in the witness box. Ask questions, respond, relax a little, and *be yourself*. Above all else, SMILE.

Smiling is the best thing you can do for yourself. Remember, this employer is looking to hire someone. That means they will be seeing the person every working day. They do not want to be around someone who is grumpy. A smile means confidence and happiness, and it is always a welcoming sign. It's hard to dislike someone who is smiling.

★ **Imagining success**

As an exercise, picture this scenario: You will be a few minutes early as you walk into the place, approach the first employee you see, and confidently say, "Hi, I'm here to see _______ ________." And they will tell you to have a seat while they let the person know you've arrived. Then you will introduce yourself to the person doing the interview. You'll smile and say your name. In all likelihood they will lead you to a private office or room and you will have a seat and the interview will begin. You are doing great, answering the questions with good examples from your previous experience, and your head is held high. You're even smiling. Toward the end you ask a few good, well-thought-out questions. The interview concludes and you stand up and shake the person's hand, thanking them for their time. You were great. Congratulations.

I'm really nervous, is that normal?

Being nervous is natural. Interviews are almost always a little intimidating for people. Don't lose your cool. If you find yourself feeling nervous, take a few deep breaths. Picture yourself after the interview is all over; feel how good it is to have done a great job in there.

Even if you've never had a job before, or you've only had a little work experience, you can still perform well in an interview. The employer thought enough of you to interview you in the first place! So, you have nothing to lose — just stay focused on the questions. You've done lots of different things in your life, so make sure you're ready to talk about them before you go in to the interview. Answer the questions enthusiastically and give examples of when you acted in that way or accomplished a similar task.

What if I'm late?

If you are late for your interview for a good reason, like the bus you were on had an accident, or there was a traffic jam due to bad weather, then tell the employer right away. Say something like:

- "I'm extremely sorry I'm late, but there was an accident . . ."

Don't dwell on it. Apologize and move on. But do give yourself lots of time to get to the interview. It's better to be really early and sit in a nearby coffee shop for half an hour than it is to be late.

If something happens at the last minute and you can't make the interview, but you still really want the job, call the employer. Tell them an emergency has come up and ask if you could possibly re-schedule your interview time.

How long do interviews last?

Some interviews last only a few minutes, while others last more than an hour. It all depends on the person, the job, and what has to be accomplished in the interview. As a general rule, most interviews are between twenty and forty minutes long.

Are all interviews the same?

No, although most are pretty similar. A standard interview is a face-to-face meeting between an employer and a candidate in a private office or area. They take the form of a discussion based on questions posed by the employer and answers given by the candidate. But sometimes employers do conduct different types of interviews. Here are a few other kinds:

Telephone Interview

One-on-one Interview

Panel Interview

Group Interview

Written interviews

Some job interviews have a written part that is conducted either before or after a normal face-to-face interview. Often the written part is an aptitude or personality-type test made up of multiple-choice questions. Some employers use these tests to help them decide who to hire. It gives them one more way to assess a candidate. Take these tests seriously and do your best. Employers who use them do so because they feel they are important.

Telephone interviews

Some organizations give interviews over the phone. Usually a phone interview means there will be more than one round of interviews. If you do well on a phone interview, it will likely be followed by a second, in-person interview.

If the phone interview is going to involve more than a few simple screening questions, then the employer will likely call you first and set up a time to call you back. This will give you time to prepare as though it were a face-to-face interview. Phone interviews can sometimes take just as long as in-person interviews, so take them seriously. Have your résumé and a pen and paper handy during the interview.

Remember, whenever you are talking to an employer on the phone, treat the conversation as an interview because you want the employer to form a good opinion of you. It may even help you to actually dress up a bit for phone interviews. Many people say it helps them "feel professional." So change out of your pajamas and put on your good clothes so you'll sound as good as you look!

Group interviews

In some cases there will be more than one candidate in the room at the same time, making the interview seem more competitive. These types of interviews are conducted for many different reasons, but **the good news is** that usually it is because the company or organization is going to be hiring more than one person, and is looking for a "team." By interviewing more than one candidate at a time, the employer can save time interviewing and also see how the successful candidates interact.

Just be yourself. Remember, if you get the job you want to be happy doing it. So act naturally, and if you are successful it should be a good fit for your personality type.

Panel interviews or multiple interviewers

In another common type of interview, more than one person will be interviewing you. There are many different reasons why employers do this. Often, employers have two people conduct the interview when the job requires a candidate who will be supervised by more than one person. Because different people have different perspectives, an employer wants to hire someone that everyone agrees will be suitable for the position.

If you find yourself in this type of interview, direct your answers to the person who asked the question, but make sure to have eye contact with both the interviewers. It is important to impress all the people in the room because when you leave, they will have a discussion based on your performance in the interview.

The truth is, you'll have to be ready for anything when you go into an interview situation. Just do your best and react positively to whatever type of interview an employer uses.

★ **TIP** **Make a good first impression. Smile. Shake the interviewer's hand firmly and make eye contact, saying, "It's nice to meet you." Don't worry if you're a little nervous. It shows that you want the job and that you are concerned about how the interview will go.**

What are some typical interview questions?

For a list of typical questions, see page 89.

What are some especially tricky questions?

For a list of tricky questions and some ways to answer them, see pages 89–91. Make sure you have prepared answers to these questions ahead of time.

When can I ask about "the money"?

It's natural to be curious about what the job pays if the wage or salary is not mentioned in the ad, or you are applying for a job that wasn't advertised. If you are expecting to be paid a wage or salary that is more than minimum wage, it's a good idea to ask about the pay at the end of the interview. If the job does not pay what you were expecting then you will avoid disappointment later. Always be polite and courteous when asking.

The best idea is to try to determine the pay range for the position before you go into an interview. This is especially true if you are applying for a job to support yourself, because you have to know how much you will need to live on. If you're in this situation, make a list of all the things you have to pay for each month and add them up. Make sure the salary for the job covers those expenses. A part-time job probably won't give you enough money if you're on your own. You may need two part-time jobs or one full-time job to make sure you can pay your rent, buy food, and pay the bills. Plus, you are going to want some left over to get other stuff — this is what will make it all worthwhile.

Be realistic with your salary expectations. Many entry-level jobs pay minimum wage or slightly higher. It is illegal for an employer to pay less than the minimum wage. (To find out the minimum wage in your province, call your ministry of labour. Look up the number in the "blue pages" section of your phone book.) Pay rates vary between communities, industries, and sectors. Ask friends who do similar jobs. Make sure the wage for the job you want is right for your situation.

When should I hand over my references?

Some employers insist that you list your references on the application form when you first apply, while others won't ask for them until the end of an interview. Not all employers check references, but most do. That's why it's best to be prepared with your references before you start your job search. Type them on a separate sheet and bring them with you to the interview.

Use only references that will speak positively about you. If you have doubts, don't use them. See pages 15–17 more information on references.

Second interviews

Sometimes, but not always, employers will call you in for a second interview. The second interview is a chance for an employer to . . .

- talk with the final few candidates one more time
- have another manager conduct the final interview
- ask different questions to help them make their decision.

Second interviews usually mean that the employer has narrowed down the hiring to two or three people. It's your chance to really shine. The employer will expect you to be really prepared. Make sure you've read any information they may have given you after the first interview. You've done very well to get this far. Good job!

How did I do? When will I find out?

One of the last questions you should ask at an interview is: "When do you anticipate making your decision?"

Sometimes an employer will take a few hours, other times a few days, maybe even weeks to make a decision about who to hire. Even if a job interview goes well, don't stop looking. There might be an even better job that comes up in the meantime. Of course it rarely happens, but the best position to be in is to have more than one job offer.

Should I make a follow-up call or write a follow-up letter?

It's up to you, but a very short letter sent by fax or e-mail is an easy way to thank the employer for the interview and re-state your interest in the position. If you decide to call, it might be a good idea to call after business hours and leave a short voice-mail message. In a thank-you message or letter it's generally not advisable to mention things you forgot to say in an interview or get into detail about why they should hire you.

Here is an example of a good follow-up note.

These days many people send a short follow-up letter. It shows that you really want the job and it is a polite way to keep your name alive in a busy employer's mind.

> **Brett Cooper**
> 4 Spruce St., Sudbury, ON P3A 2K4
> (705) 555-1818
>
> October 5, 2000
> Robert Arnold
> Manager, Office Co. Ltd.
> 4 Regent St.,
> Sudbury, ON P3E 4A2
>
> Dear Mr. Arnold:
>
> Just a short note to thank you for my interview yesterday. I enjoyed meeting you. I remain very interested in the ____________________ position and look forward to hearing from you soon.
>
> Sincerely,
>
> Brett Cooper

I don't think it's the right job for me

What do you do if over the course of an interview you realize that you don't want the job? Perhaps it involves longer hours than you were expecting, or the location is too difficult or costly to get to, or the wage is far too low, or the job itself is not what you were expecting at all. First of all, because no one wants to turn down a job and regret it later, it's a good idea to talk something like this over with someone you trust. Tell them your concerns, what's bugging you about it. Try to make a firm decision about whether or not you want the job. Perhaps you'll take it and give it a try, or take it for now but keep looking for something more suitable. If you do decide to take the job, then great.

If you've decided against it, then it's polite to let the employer know that you are withdrawing your application, because someone else out there probably really wants the job and is waiting to find out. You could call the employer and let them know, or else e-mail or fax them a short note.

I got the job!

Accepting the position is the next big step. When an employer calls to offer you a job you should already have decided what you are going to say. If it's yes, then congratulations. But in the excitement, don't forget to clarify a few things before you accept:

What does the job pay?
When do you start?
Who do you report to on the first day?
How long are the workdays or shifts?
What is your schedule for the first week?
Is there a dress code or uniform?

I didn't get the job . . .

If you had an interview but didn't get the job, an employer will sometimes call and let you know. Other times, they will send you a letter. They won't say very much, and probably won't really tell you why — even if you ask — so if they call, just keep the conversation short.

The important thing is to not lose heart. It happens to everyone many times over the course of a lifetime. Why people choose one person over another is sometimes hard to understand. It's okay and really normal to be disappointed, but move on quickly. Don't let it get to you. Just the fact that you got an interview means there is something special about you. If one employer thought so, others will too. Getting an interview is a success in itself. There are many great jobs out there for you. So what are you waiting for?

DO'S AND DON'TS OF INTERVIEWS

✓
- ***Do make a good first impression.***
- ***Do smile.***
- ***Do imagine success.***
- ***Do be ready to face any type of interview.***
- ***Do bring along two fresh copies of your résumé and your reference sheet. Do research the position and find out the salary range before you apply.***

✗
- ***Don't ask about "the money" until the end of the interview.***

Where to get more help for your interview

Knowing how to be successful in an interview can be difficult when you're starting out. Almost everyone has been where you are at some point and knows how difficult it can be. Ask a teacher, guidance counsellor, family member, or youth worker for advice, or seek out professionals at youth employment centres who can help you work on your interview skills. Check out chapter 10 for help in finding a centre near you.

9

Success on the Job

"How will I know what to do?"

Congratulations on your new job! Let's take a look at what you should know and what you can expect from your new job. You want to do a great job for many reasons, like . . .

- you don't want to have to look for another one soon!
- you want to work to make the money you need
- you want to do well so when it's time to get another job, you'll have good references, you'll have learned a lot, and you'll have gained experience.

I'm nervous about my first day . . .

Everyone gets nervous about their first day. Just make sure you . . .

- set your alarm clock
- get up on time
- leave early, giving yourself lots of time to get there ten minutes before you are supposed to start
- bring something to eat, or some money to buy food if there is somewhere nearby to do so

- choose what you want to wear the night before
- know exactly how to get to your new job
- know who you are reporting to.

What can I expect on my first day on the job?

Your new boss will expect you to be there on time and ready to start. You will probably have training on the first day. Sometimes this means you will learn from the person who was in the position before you, or another staff member — or even the boss — may be in charge of training you.

You won't be expected to learn it all in one day, but be eager to learn all that the job requires. Depending on what the job is, it'll take some time to get good at it. Pay attention to everything you are told, and don't be afraid to ask questions. At the beginning it's better to ask a lot of questions than to do a task incorrectly and have to re-do it. Taking notes can be very helpful if it's the sort of job where there are lots of details to remember.

★ **TIP Be ready for anything and be flexible. It may be hard to remember everything, but you will learn it all in time.**

You will also meet new people. At the beginning, you probably won't be able to remember everyone's name, their roles, and how they might affect you and your job. Remember, everyone had a first day once too. Co-workers are going to ask you about yourself, so be prepared to smile and say a few words about where you've come from or what you've been doing up to this point. People are always curious about someone new. You'll be spending a lot of time with these people, so be friendly without talking too much. It's best to save your long conversations for the breaks, lunch, or after work.

What should I wear?

When you went to your interview, did you get a chance to see what other people were wearing? Was there a dress code or a uniform? If so, your employer probably told you about it when you were offered the job. If not, then dress as nicely as you can and be prepared to find out more on your first day. Remember, you're not expected to know it all from day one, so just dress neatly and comfortably. You'll feel a lot better about it tomorrow when you know more about what's expected of you.

Do I get a break?

Yes, of course you get a break. But people are often busy at work and may forget to tell you about it. So during your training on the first day, make sure you remember to ask your boss or a co-worker when the breaks are and whether or not you are paid for that time. These aren't dumb questions, since breaks differ from workplace to workplace. Don't let the issue slide by because you are too shy to ask.

Make sure you return from your break on time. Your boss and co-workers depend on you to be punctual.

★ **TIP** **An employer must give you a break to eat, even if you are working a part-time shift. If you find you're not getting breaks, ask your supervisor about the best time to take your breaks. If the response is not satisfactory, call your local ministry of labour (look in the "blue pages" of your phone book) and find out your rights when it comes to breaks. It is very important that you be allowed to stop work and take a break, eat, and use the washroom.**

What if I've never done this task before?

Every new job will involve some tasks that you've never done before. Just be honest and tell the person training you that this is new to you. Ask them to show you how it's done first. Don't guess. You'll pick it up. Never be afraid to ask for help. Be as flexible in the beginning as you can.

When do I get paid?

Every company and organization has a different pay schedule. Most pay bi-weekly, which means one paycheque every two weeks (for example, a cheque every second Friday). Others pay semi-monthly, which means two paycheques per month (for example, a cheque on the first of the month and another on the fifteenth). Ask about when your first paycheque will arrive. It's important to be prepared and to make sure you can make your money last.

These days, many companies can pay you by direct deposit. This means they will electronically deposit your money directly into your bank account. To do this you will need to open a bank account and give them a blank cheque with the word "VOID" written across it, or they will need your savings account number and your branch number. This is the fastest and easiest way to get your paycheque. Your employer will still give you a paper record of the deposit as proof that you've been paid.

Other companies prefer to give you an actual cheque for you to deposit. Make sure you check with your bank to see if there is a holding period on cheques deposited in your account by an ATM. If there is you might have to wait a week before you can get at your money. Talk to your bank and they will tell you your options regarding depositing cheques.

If you have questions about taxes and deductions, see pages 113–14 for more information.

★ **TIP** One thing you can do after a little while is ask to see the company's human resources policies and procedures information (sometimes called a "procedures manual") — if they haven't already given it to you to read. Not every workplace will have a policy manual, especially if the company is small, but many do. In the manual you will find the company's rules concerning sick days, leave, benefits, pay days, harassment complaint procedures, dress code rules, vacation time, and many other rules and regulations the company has set out for its employees.

A company's **HUMAN RESOURCES** or **PERSONNEL** department is in charge of policies and procedures concerning the employees in the company. It often takes care of things like hiring staff, booking vacation time, payroll, sick days, leaves of absence, firing, and benefits packages. It is a good place to go if you need information or have a question or concern.

What are "commission" and "base pay"?

If you are working at a job that involves selling, you will probably need to know about commission. Commission pay is based on what, and how much, you sell. Usually sales jobs also have a "base pay." Base pay is an hourly wage that you earn no matter how much you sell, and the commission is the money you make on top of this. Many great sales jobs have some commission or "bonus pay" attached to them to give you incentive to work hard, sell lots, and do a good job.

When is commission not a good idea?

Some people are very good at sales and they make a lot of money, but they know how to do it and have a lot of experience. If you've never sold before, be careful of 100% commission jobs. You might work a whole week, not sell anything, and therefore not get paid. Accept that selling is hard if you've never done it before, and that at the beginning you will probably not make the thousands of dollars a week that they say you can. It may take time to get that good at it. If you want a sales job, start by taking one that has base pay plus commission, just to be safe, and make sure you understand and agree to how the pay system works before you start.

I didn't realize what sales involved . . .

Sometimes young people take sales jobs, only to find that they aren't good at it or don't like it. Often this is because jobs that involve direct selling, either over the phone or door to door, pay by commission only. The uncertainty this causes about how much they will get paid is sometimes too risky for young people. Other times they don't like the pressure. If you're good at sales then you will know right away and you'll likely do very well. If you find sales isn't for you, then begin a new job search as quickly as possible. It's good to discover what you like and dislike in the working world. It will help you make better decisions in the future.

What if I'm sick or need time off?

If you wake up one morning and find that you're sick and are unable to make it into work, then you must call your boss as soon as he or she arrives at work. Try not to leave voice mail — do your best to talk to them directly and tell them what's wrong with you and why you won't be in. Depending on the province you live in, the kind of job you have, and the company you work for, you may not be paid for sick days. This is especially true at the beginning of your employment period.

Everyone gets sick and has to take the occasional day off work. If it's serious and you are going to need several days off, talk to your boss. You will probably have to get a note from your doctor.

If you need some time off, say a few hours, to go to a doctor's appointment, or to register for school, or some other important engagement, then make sure you ask your employer well in advance. Most employers realize that things come up, and are happy to work around them. Just don't leave it to the last minute to tell your supervisor. You don't want to leave them understaffed.

Is this job safe?

Never agree to do a task that you feel is dangerous or unsafe. Instead, tell your employer that you feel the task is dangerous. Show them why. Try to work something out. Most employers will never put you in danger on purpose. If you are having a problem in this area, then call the ministry of labour in your province. You can find their number in the "blue pages" section of your phone book.

What are payroll taxes and deductions?

When you started your job, you should have filled out a form that tells the employer how much tax to take off your paycheque. Unless you are a student and you checked off the box saying you will not make the minimum amount this year to have tax deducted, your cheque will have less on it than you might be expecting.

Working out how much tax is being taken off can be a little tricky, and these days it's often done by computer programs, so just ask your employer to explain the various deductions.

In addition to tax, there will also be deductions made for the Canada Pension Plan (CPP), Employment Insurance (EI), and if you're in a union, union dues. Some companies also make other deductions for health plans or, if you've requested it, RRSP contributions. Just ask your boss or the person on payroll to go over your pay stub with you. If there are deductions being made, then they must be listed on your pay stub.

While you are working you are also entitled to earn vacation pay for every hour you work. Depending on your job, some employers pay this on every cheque; others let it build up. Make sure to ask for your vacation pay when you leave.

★ **TIP** **If you are receiving your wages in cash and there are no tax deductions being made, you might be getting paid illegally. This is often called getting paid "under the table." It is against the law not to pay tax. You also may not be on record as an employee, which might mean you won't have rights if you are hurt at work, or you want to take a vacation, or any of the other things that are provided under the law for people who work in Canada. Talk to your employer and find out if they are making tax deductions. Make sure they are paying you legally. If you have any concerns, talk to your parents, or call the ministry of labour in your province (the number is in the "blue pages" section of your phone book).**

It's best not to discuss your salary, wage, or deductions with other staff members or colleagues until you've been there a while. Keep it between you and your boss or supervisor at the beginning. People do not tend to show their pay stubs to other workers because it is private information, and knowing what others get paid can lead to bad feelings. Use your own judgement, but in most cases your salary is a matter for you and your employer to discuss.

What happens if I find myself in a job I think is a scam?

If you find yourself doing a job that makes you very upset or uncomfortable, then it's okay to look for another job. If doing a job makes you act or treat other people in a way that is unfair or misleading, even illegal, then quit.

If you are concerned about a job being "for real," then ask someone you trust, like a parent or teacher or friend, for advice. Tell them you're worried the job is not everything they say it is. Ask them to help you decide what to do. Don't be embarrassed. Don't keep it to yourself.

What is a performance evaluation?

Most employers will have periodic meetings with you to discuss your job performance. Together you will review your performance on the job and discuss any improvements that need to be made. It is a good time to let your boss know about any problems you are having at work, or any expectations you feel are unrealistic. These meetings usually happen after the first three months, then possibly again after six months or a year. (See the section on probation on page 120.)

Getting feedback about your performance on the job helps you to do a better job and improve as you go. It's important to ask, every now and then, "How am I doing?" Feedback is especially important at the beginning of a job. Ask how you are doing, and whether you can do better somehow. Take the criticism in a good way. It will help you do better and succeed.

What are my rights on the job?

As an employee working in Canada your rights are protected under the law. If you are experiencing harassment, unsafe work conditions, unfair pay, mistreatment, discrimination, or abuse on the job, then speak up. Tell someone you trust what is going on at work. Don't keep quiet. You're not alone and it's not your fault. Your employer and colleagues are not allowed to mistreat you at work.

If you don't have anyone to talk to, call your provincial ministry of labour and ask them for advice. You won't have to give your name or tell them the employer's name to get advice. Your rights are protected under the law.

What's a union?

Unions are organizations that look after and protect the interests of workers. If you get a job in a company that has a union, you may be required to become a member. If you do, and you have questions about what role your union plays in your workplace, make sure you ask your union representative whatever is on your mind.

Relationships with co-workers and employers

A good working relationship with your boss, co-workers, and other staff is worth developing right from the start. You'll be spending every workday with these people, so you'll need to get along well together. Start things off on the right foot. When you meet them, take some time to ask them a question or two about what they do at work and what their job entails. Always be polite and courteous.

You may not become great friends with everyone you work with, but that's fine — you're not expected to. What's important is to strike a balance. A good working relationship means that you can work with someone in a way that is friendly, professional, and respectful.

If you find you're having a problem with a co-worker, try talking to them about it. Make sure you pick a good time when it's not too busy at work. Don't yell or get angry. Tell them how you are feeling and why. Don't blame or accuse them. Simply address the specific problem you've been having. Be polite but firm and try to offer a solution. Try asking something like:

- "I don't understand why you got angry with me over ____________________."
- "I would really like to try and work together better. How can I improve things?"

If talking to your co-worker doesn't seem to change anything, or they don't respond in a favourable way, then it's time to take a moment and speak to your boss about the problem.

Try to resolve work problems when they arise. Don't let them sit and get worse.

DO'S OF WORKPLACE RELATIONSHIPS

- ***Do be honest and direct in your communication.***
- ***Do go first to the person with whom you are having the problem. If you are unsuccessful, then go to your supervisor.***
- ***Do try to resolve the issue right away.***
- ***Do speak honestly with your supervisor if the problem is with them.***
- ***Do listen carefully to the other person's point of view. They may have good reasons for their behaviour.***

I'm having a really big problem . . .

Trust your instincts. Occasionally people have bad experiences at work. If you're experiencing discrimination or harassment at work by a co-worker, then speak to your boss immediately. If you can't, or it's your boss who is the problem, talk to someone you trust. Tell them what's happening to you, even if you're not sure it is discrimination or harassment.

Don't keep it a secret or blame yourself. When something is seriously wrong, when someone is not treating you the right way, do something about it. It's just going to get worse if you keep it to yourself.

Checklist — My Summer Job Is Ending

If it's almost September and you're going back to school, don't forget the following:

- **Ask your employer for a letter of reference (see pages 14–17).**
- **Ask how you go about getting hired next summer, if that's something you might want.**
- **Find out if they need part-time or occasional help during the school year. You might need some money near the holidays.**
- **Make sure you leave your address with the employer in case there is vacation pay or a final paycheque still to come after you're finished.**

Should I ask for a letter of reference?

Although most future employers will want to actually speak to your last employer on the phone when they are checking your references, it's always nice insurance to have a written letter of reference. If a company goes out of business, or you lose contact with a former boss because they move or leave the company, a letter is some proof that you did a good job and were a good employee. Letters of reference are also helpful if you move from one city or town to another.

I'm out of here!

People leave jobs for many reasons. If you are thinking of quitting, make sure you give at least two weeks' notice. Depending on the situation, you might think it's polite to give your boss more notice. People understand that everyone has to move on to new jobs, or go back to school, or go travelling at some point, so just make sure you are courteous and give enough notice. You will likely need the employer to be a reference for your next job search, even if it isn't going to be soon.

Many young people work in shops or restaurants where work is done in shifts. One of the risks of giving two weeks' notice in those positions is that people find they get fewer shifts than they'd like in the final two weeks of work. It's up to you how you want to deal with your specific situation, but usually if you treat people with respect and give them fair notice, then they will return the respect. By the time you are ready to leave you will probably know if this is true of your employer.

My contract's ending . . .

Many jobs are called contract positions. This means you agree to work for a specific amount of time, such as several weeks, three months, six months, or a year. Contracts are a great way to get your foot in the door and get full-time work experience. And they may even lead to a permanent position.

But eventually the contract will end, and if there is no way the company or organization can keep you on, it's time for you to start looking for another position. If you're finding it hard to get another job right away and you need money for rent and food, you may be eligible to collect Employment Insurance (EI). To find out if you qualify, call Human Resources Development Canada by looking up "employment insurance" in the "blue pages" of the phone book.

If you know your contract is going to end, try to plan ahead. Now that you've been working, you have a whole new set of contacts. Start your job search before the contract is over. Let everyone you've met in your job know that your contract is unfortunately ending and that you'll be looking for a new position soon. Ask them to let you know if they hear of any openings at other companies.

I've been "let go." What happens now?

There are many reasons why people are "let go." Sometimes companies "lay people off" because they are cutting back on staff. Other times workers are fired.

Whether you've been let go because of cutbacks or because you've been fired, it's an awful feeling if you didn't see it coming. Take some time to reflect on why you were let go and what this means to you. Were you happy in your job? Do you want to change jobs or look for another similar job? You will have many questions. Try to talk about your situation with someone you trust. Make some plans for the future, both short-term and long-term. It's likely to be a difficult time for you now but it will pass, and you will find another position soon. The sooner you begin looking, the better.

If you are being fired after your probation period is over, the employer must tell you why. Make sure it's a legitimate reason. If it's something you did or failed to do, then make sure you get it in writing. Depending on how long you've worked there, it shouldn't be the first time you're hearing about it. If you have questions or concerns about why you were fired, then call your local ministry of labour (their phone number is in the "blue pages" section of the phone book).

PROBATION PERIOD is the period of time at the beginning of a job when you and the employer can decide if you are a good match for the position. Probation periods often last three months, but could be shorter or longer — be sure to find out when yours ends.

TIP If you suspect you are not doing a good job, and you are worried about losing your job, talk to your employer about it. Ask for more training, guidance, and feedback. You may be able to correct the problem before it gets too bad.

One of the main reasons people lose their jobs is because they have poor personal skills to be able to deal with others in the workplace. Communication problems feature in most dismissals. Other common reasons include an inability to do the job, refusal to do a task, theft, breaking a contract, ongoing lateness or being absent or unreliable, and misconduct. Take every step available to you to do a good job. Know what is expected of you. Read your job description carefully, ask questions, and try to exceed the basic requirements.

I think I need more training or qualifications . . .

You will soon find out that training and learning never stop. Just because you might have finished school, or dropped out of school, it doesn't mean that you won't want to upgrade your skills to earn more money or get a better job. Many employers encourage their staff to take night school, community college courses, or even university courses to gain more knowledge if it will help them on the job. They will often pay for some of it too. Ask your boss or the person in charge of human resources in your company if the company is willing to pay for some or all of a course you'd like to take.

One thing to consider is that if the employer does pay, you may have to agree to stay with the company for a certain amount of time following the course. Is this what you want? If so, then great. If you want to go back to school to upgrade your skills so you can get a better job somewhere else, then it's best to try to pay for it yourself. An employer will be unlikely to give you a good reference if they pay for your courses and then you take your new skills somewhere else.

I'd like to go back to school full-time

It's always a good idea to return to school if you didn't finish high school or would like to do some post-secondary courses. School diplomas give you access to better jobs later — jobs that pay more, jobs that will give you opportunity for promotion, jobs that are more interesting to go to every day. School *now* is a great way to get what you want *later* in life. Stay in it for as long as you can.

10

More Help

"I still have more questions."

While this book will give you the basics of how to do a job search, you probably still have more questions. Try asking an employment counsellor at your local employment resource or training centre.

What's an employment counsellor or employment centre?

Employment counsellors are people who work in your community helping youth like you find jobs. In some provinces they deliver government-sponsored programs, and in others they work for community agencies.

The agencies and governments they work for might vary across Canada but what they do is very similar — simply put, they help people like you with their job searches. Most of the services are free and they get great results. Sometimes they have actual job listings, too. So if you're having trouble finding a job, go to your local employment centre and make an appointment to see a youth employment counsellor. It's a great step to take.

How can I find the one nearest me?

There are hundreds of agencies that provide employment counselling across Canada. Here are some ways to find the one nearest you:

1. **Look up "employment," "careers," or "youth" in the yellow pages. See if there are any community agencies that provide employment or career counselling services.**
2. **Go to your local library or community/recreation centre and ask the librarian or community worker if they have any resource materials that list nearby youth employment services or centres.**
3. **Call or visit the Human Resources Centre of Canada nearest you and ask if they can refer you to a youth employment counsellor in the community. They usually have lots of information in their centres on bulletin boards and tables. You can find their number in the government "blue pages" section of the phone book.**
4. **Do a search on the Internet or check out one of the sites on pages 125–28. Find a link to your community and the phone numbers of any employment centres near you.**
5. **Ask your school guidance counsellor if they know where you can get job search help.**
6. **If you are collecting social assistance or welfare, then ask your worker to refer you to a youth employment organization or program.**

What kinds of services does an employment centre provide?

Most employment centres have free services like faxing, photocopying, Internet access, job listings, computers, résumé and interview counselling, referral information, entrepreneurship programs, and access to government programs designed to give you a start in the workforce. They can link you up with apprenticeship programs, internships, wage subsidy programs, and free training. Most of all, they'll give you some good advice about your specific job search.

Web sites

Youth and Employment — General Sites

The Canadian Job Hunt Page
Lots of links to job listings, job banks, job search resources, and résumé services http://www.studentsguide.com/jobs/

Human Resources Development Canada Youth Site
Links to different federal government youth employment initiatives http://youth.hrdc-drhc.gc.ca/

Ontario Association of Youth Employment Centres (OAYEC)
Names and addresses of youth employment centres across Ontario http://www.interlog.com/~oayec

Youth Employment Service (Y.E.S.) Toronto
Canada's oldest youth employment centre, located in downtown Toronto Tel: (416) 504-5516 http://www.yes.on.ca

Youth Link
Work experience and summer jobs, learning opportunities, and career planning information
http://youth.hrdc-drhc.gc.ca/ythlink/ythlink.shtml

Youth Resource Network Canada
General federal government web site with links to many sites across Canada Tel: 1 800 935-5555 http://youth.gc.ca/

Aboriginal Youth and Employment

Aboriginal Youth Network — Employment Centre
http://www.ayn.ca/employment/employ_mainpage.htm

Apprenticeship Information

Canadian Council of Directors of Apprenticeship
http://www.hrdc-drhc.gc.ca/hrib/hrp-prh/redseal/redconte.html

Industry Training & Apprenticeship Commission
http://www.itac.gov.bc.ca/otherapp.htm

Disability and Employment

Ability OnLine Support Network
http://www.ablelink.org

Canadian Association of Independent Living Centres
http://www.cailc.ca/links.htm

Lesbian, Gay, Bisexual, Transgendered Resources

GayCanada
List by city/province of organizations and resources serving LGBT youth http://www.gaycanada.com/categories/youth.htm

Provincial Government Employment Sites

Alberta
http://www.aecd.gov.ab.ca/hre/programsServices/youthConnections/YOUTH.htm

British Columbia
http://www.youth.gov.bc.ca/

Manitoba
http://www.edu.gov.mb.ca/tce/carjob/carjob.html

New Brunswick
http://www.gov.nb.ca/hrd/ythdir.htm

Newfoundland and Labrador
http://www.gov.nf.ca/nlwin/HOME/FHOME.HTM

Northwest Territories
http://siksik.learnnet.nt.ca/index.html

Nova Scotia
http://www.gov.ns.ca/ecor/infocent/employ.htm

Nunavut
http://www.gov.nu.ca/

Ontario
http://youthjobs.gov.on.ca/index.html

Prince Edward Island
http://www2.gov.pe.ca/InfoPEI/Education_and_Learning/Youth_Programs/

Quebec
http://www.jeunes.gouv.qc.ca/

Saskatchewan
http://www.sasked.gov.sk.ca/jobstart/content.html#1

Yukon
http://www.gov.yk.ca/depts/dgs/yukonhire/

Provincial Ministries of Labour

Links to each province's ministry of labour
http://info.load-otea.hrdc-drhc.gc.ca/~lsweb/proven.htm

Volunteering Information

Charity Village
http://www.charityvillage.com

Volunteer Canada
http://www.volunteer.ca